Secrets of the Prince of Expositors

Secrets of the Prince of Expositors

Applying the Bible like Alexander Maclaren

Michael Hawk Mills

Foreword by David L. Allen

WIPF & STOCK · Eugene, Oregon

SECRETS OF THE PRINCE OF EXPOSITORS
Applying the Bible like Alexander Maclaren

Copyright © 2025 Michael Hawk Mills. All rights reserved. Except for brief quotations in critical publications or reviews, no part of this book may be reproduced in any manner without prior written permission from the publisher. Write: Permissions, Wipf and Stock Publishers, 199 W. 8th Ave., Suite 3, Eugene, OR 97401.

Wipf & Stock
An Imprint of Wipf and Stock Publishers
199 W. 8th Ave., Suite 3
Eugene, OR 97401

www.wipfandstock.com

PAPERBACK ISBN: 979-8-3852-3620-6
HARDCOVER ISBN: 979-8-3852-3621-3
EBOOK ISBN: 979-8-3852-3622-0

VERSION NUMBER 11/14/25

This book is dedicated to my father, David Mills. Thank you for supporting me and for sacrificing your time to help make this work possible.

Contents

Foreword by David L. Allen | ix
Preface | xi
Introduction: The Neglect of Biblical Application | xv

1 Life Lessons and Preaching Practices | 1
2 Pictures and Models: Narratives | 22
3 Shadows of What Is to Come: Law | 41
4 Prayers of the Saints: The Psalms | 59
5 Proper Living: Wisdom Literature | 77
6 Proclaiming the Word: Prophecy and Epistles | 95
7 Conclusion | 114

Appendix: "An Old Preacher on Preaching" | 121
Bibliography | 137

Foreword
by David L. Allen

WHILE CHARLES SPURGEON IS often regarded as the greatest expository preacher of 19th-century Victorian England, many are unaware that he was, in fact, eclipsed by another towering figure—someone who was a more consistent and meticulous practitioner of expository preaching: Alexander Maclaren. For forty-five years, Maclaren held court from the pulpit of Union Chapel in Manchester, where his sermons made an indelible mark on the landscape of Christian preaching. His influence in both England and America cannot be overstated, and his legacy lives on through his monumental work *Expositions of Holy Scripture*, which continues to shape the preaching of today.

What set Maclaren apart as the premier expositor of his time was his unwavering commitment to following the structure of the biblical text. He was diligent in studying each passage's original Hebrew or Greek, spending countless hours in sermon preparation—some say up to sixty hours for a single message. His discipline in exegesis was paired with a deep understanding of the text's literary and historical context, which he skillfully wove into his sermons using illustrations and applications that resonated with his audience. His approach was methodical yet engaging, and his influence was felt across both sides of the Atlantic.

W. Robertson Nicoll once remarked, "A man who reads one of Maclaren's sermons must either take his outline—or take another text." This speaks to Maclaren's unparalleled ability to mine the depths of Scripture and present it with such clarity and insight that it was nearly impossible for others to follow him without the same rigorous commitment.

What makes Maclaren's example so valuable for us today is his ability to balance two essential aspects of preaching: a rigorous commitment to the faithful exposition of Scripture and a deep concern for its relevance to contemporary life. In a world that often swings between these two extremes, Maclaren's ministry serves as a model for preachers who seek to honor the text while also addressing the pressing issues of their hearers.

In this work, Dr. Michael Mills offers us a thoughtful and insightful introduction to Alexander Maclaren—not merely as a preacher but as a man of deep personal holiness and a theologian of preaching. More than a biography, this book sheds light on the theological foundations of Maclaren's ministry and the principles that governed his approach to expository preaching. It is a study of a man whose legacy has been cemented as one of the great expository preachers in the history of the church.

Every pastor who reads this book will find his heart warmed, his ministry strengthened, and his preaching elevated. There is much to learn from Maclaren's life and legacy. I trust this work will inspire many to follow in his footsteps and embrace the timeless art of expository preaching.

Preface

I FIRST BECAME INTERESTED in Alexander Maclaren when I came across some of his sermons while doing research for the daunting task of selecting a dissertation topic. I was impressed by Maclaren's sermons and by the number of authors who lauded him for his expositional preaching. However, recent scholarship has not studied his methods of exposition in any depth. The mystery of Alexander Maclaren intensified for me during a visit to England. Not long after Maclaren passed away, his library and other artifacts were largely lost, except for a small box of sermon outlines and letters that are stored in Oxford. These objects contradicted some of the claims made by homiletical scholars regarding Maclaren. Thus began my desire to examine the life and sermons of this master preacher and learn why so many consider him to be the prince of expositors.

I floated the possibility of studying Maclaren to my PhD supervisor Matthew McKellar as well as others in the preaching department. The reaction from my professors was shockingly positive. They immediately recognized the need for contemporary studies on Maclaren in light of a resurgence in expository preaching studies, especially expository preaching in its purest form, known as text-driven preaching. Text-driven preaching seeks to re-echo the substances, structure, and spirit of the text in the sermon. While Alexander Maclaren cannot be described as a pure text-driven preacher, he was certainly closer in substance and style than many others including the great homiletician Charles H. Spurgeon. Many preachers in Maclaren's day, much like some preachers today, used the biblical text merely as a means of starting their sermon. However, the points of the sermon were not derived from the structure or substance of the text itself. Rather, they derived their sermon points from their own minds. Maclaren

Preface

stood out for keeping his sermons much more closely to the substances, spirit, and structure of the biblical text. My dissertation work focused on Maclaren's preaching and applications from the Old Testament.

By God's providence, my research into Maclaren gained the attention of Thomas Nelson Bible Publishing, who wanted to created a new *Alexander Maclaren Study Bible*. I agreed to serve as the general editor, and my studies of Maclaren's applications expanded to the whole of Scripture. This endeavor confirmed my admiration for Maclaren and his preaching from the Bible. He has greatly influenced me as an individual and an expositor, and I wish to share his practices so others can be moved by the prince of expositors as well.

I am grateful for those who have poured into my life over the last several years as I grew in the Lord and learned what it means to accurately divide the word of truth. Matthew McKellar, my PhD supervising professor, is an encouragement both in and outside the classroom. His concern for my life and ministry is noticeable through our conversations together. He challenged me and provided invaluable insight throughout this process. David Allen has also been instrumental in getting my research on Maclaren published. This work would not be here today if not for his uplifting words and sacrificial help.

I have several family members who stood by me on this journey. My mother was a keen source of encouragement when living away from home, especially during the rough seasons. Also, I want to thank my brother for the time he spent reading and critiquing this project. His feedback has been invaluable throughout this process. My father stimulated my desire to ask deeper questions and grow. He was a continuous motivation to work hard for the glory of God. He has spent untold hours reading manuscripts, giving editorial advice, and challenging my thoughts and opinions. He has made me both a better writer, a better scholar, and a better person.

I am especially grateful to my wife, Ashley, for her support all these years. She lived in houses she did not like, worked jobs she did not enjoy, and edited enumerable pages of research documents for me. She even gave up several of her Saturdays to help me find and organize research materials. Anything good from this book can be attributed to her hard work and to God's constant provision. I am thankful for your love and look forward to what God has in store for us in the future.

Preface

Finally, I want to give glory to God. He has sustained and strengthened me every step of the way. I could not have done this without him. To him be the glory.

Michael Hawk Mills
Ashville, Alabama
December 2024

Ardfern, CC BY-SA 4.0, via Wikimedia Commons

Introduction

The Neglect of Biblical Application

"Shame on us preachers if we have made a living Gospel into a dead theology."
—ALEXANDER MACLAREN

CROWDS THRONGED TO HEAR Alexander Maclaren. Even after building a larger sanctuary, people had to bribe the doormen for a seat, and chairs were placed on the stage surrounding the pulpit. What drew so many to Alexander Maclaren? For one, he knew how to apply the text to real life. In an era when most preachers called themselves expositors because their sermons merely began with a text, Maclaren stood apart because he devoted his sermons solely to dividing, explaining, and enforcing a text within its literary and historical context. His dedication to the exposition of Scripture surpassed that of his friend Charles H. Spurgeon and caused his popularity as a preacher to rival Spurgeon's. Insightful application from the biblical text itself marked Maclaren as unique, and people longed to hear his preaching for that reason.

Alexander Maclaren is best known as the pastor of Union Chapel in Manchester, England, from 1858 until 1903. He is considered by many to be one of the top five English preachers of the Victorian era. After his retirement, he published a collection of his sermons titled *Expositions of Holy Scripture* which has been widely read, studied, and praised for decades. Blackwood calls him "the prince of expositors."[1] Carlile wrote, "It is safe to say that no man of our time in the department of Biblical exposition

1. Blackwood, *Expository Preaching for Today*, 14.

INTRODUCTION

has laid Christians under greater obligations, and the teachers who do not know his writings can hardly be described as well read."[2] Dargan claims Maclaren's sermons were the most widely read behind Spurgeon's in the early twentieth century.[3] Moyer wrote in 1962, "Maclaren's sermons have, perhaps next to Spurgeon's, been the most widely read sermons of their time, and are still greatly appreciated."[4] More recently, Pace comments that Maclaren "is generally regarded as one of the most prolific expositors in the history of the Christian pulpit."[5] Larsen likewise says, "No sermons from the nineteenth century are so thoroughly worth reading as Maclaren's."[6] Lastly, Wiersbe argues that preachers could improve their preaching simply by reading Maclaren's sermons, and he credits Maclaren as being one of the biggest influences in his own preaching.[7] Preachers today need to study how this master expositor preached across various parts of the Holy Scriptures—especially considering the great difficulty the preacher faces when trying to make applications that are truly text-driven.

Maclaren's ministry remains as a needed model for today because countless congregants still see the Bible as stories with little or no relevance to their daily duties. Every Sunday people go to a Bible study, listen to a sermon, or read the Bible; yet they leave without transforming any part of their lives. They pick up the Book, but their life rarely changes. Despite consistently studying the Bible, some people show little difference between the way they act now and the way they acted years ago. This problem partially can be narrowed down to a lack of good biblical application coming from preachers in the pulpit. Maclaren, on the other hand, can show today's preachers how to make the Bible's truths come alive and applicable.

BIBLICAL APPLICATION: DEFINITION, DANGERS, AND DILEMMA

What is *biblical application*? One way to describe biblical application is the process of taking a passage from the Bible and discovering how it personally and practically informs what one does in life. Application is personal

2. Carlile, *Alexander Maclaren, D.D.*, 134.
3. Dargan, *A History of Preaching*, vol. 2, 576.
4. Moyer, *Who Was Who in Church History*, 267.
5. Pace, "Alexander Maclaren," 70.
6. Larsen, *The Company of Preachers*, 582.
7. Wiersbe, *Walking with the Giants*, 226 and 228.

Introduction

because it is focused on people's personal lives, and application is practical because it is not an abstract idea but something concrete that people can actually do. If people know the facts of the Bible, but they are unable to connect the Bible to their lives in a way that is both personal and practical, then they have missed the crucial step of biblical application.

This definition is crucial for preachers to understand because true exposition involves not only explaining a text but applying it to one's audience. Chappell argues, "Application justifies exposition. . . . Until we apply a truth, understanding of it remains incomplete. This means that until a preacher provides application, exposition remains incomplete."[8] Vines and Shaddix also observe,

> Just because the preacher explains the text clearly and makes a convincing argument does not necessarily mean the listeners will make the connection between the biblical text and their lives. To be sure, the Bible is relevant regardless of what people may think. But the Bible's being relevant does not guarantee that every person understands its relevancy. The responsibility of the preacher, then, is to establish that relevancy in the minds of his listeners through application.[9]

Application helps the audience understand how the text can change their lives in the power of the Holy Spirit.[10] In fact, change is the purpose of application. Application is done with the intent that people, churches, families, and communities are conformed into the image of Christ by the grace of God through the power of the Holy Spirit.

The need for sermon applications does not eliminate the potential pitfalls expositors face, however, when attempting to apply a text to their hearers. Preachers and teachers alike may easily eisegete or import meaning into a verse of Scripture which is not part of the original author's intent. Robinson calls this the "heresy of application." Robinson states that many pastors

> may not have learned how to make the journey from the biblical text to the modern world. They get out of seminary and realize the preacher's question is application: How do you take this text and determine what it means for this audience? Sometimes we apply the text in ways that might make the biblical writer say, "Wait a

---

8. Chapell. *Christ-Centered Preaching*, 211.
9. Vines and Shaddix, *Power in the Pulpit*, 181.
10. Chapell, *Christ-Centered Preaching*, 213.

Introduction

minute, that's the wrong use of what I said." This is the heresy of a good truth applied in the wrong way.[11]

Incorrectly applying the Bible can lead congregants to believe a verse teaches a truth which the inspired author did not mean for it to teach.

Because of this danger, preachers and teachers often are tempted to substitute genuine biblical applications for something else in their lessons. First, we substitute understanding how a passage was applied to the original audience for how the passage should be applied to us now. We are happy to reprimand Israel or the early church for poor behavior, but then we go home and never talk about how the passage also applies to our behavior today.

Second, we substitute affirming doctrinal truths for changing behavior. Scripture teaches that theological study is pointless if it does not lead to conformity to Christ.[12] Simply explaining a doctrine is not the same as making application because it is possible to believe the Christian truths intellectually and still live a very unChristian life.

Third, we substitute a generic call for obedience instead of listing specific areas for obedience. Many preachers feel like they have applied the Bible because they have told people to obey God. However, the command to obey God is so broad that it is possible for audiences to feel as if they have applied the text to their lives while simultaneously ignoring specific areas where they need to improve. Paul gives a great example of how to avoid this substitution in Ephesians 4 where his general call to obedience in verses 20 through 24 are followed by specific examples of obedience in verses 25 through 32.

Fourth, we substitute applying the Bible to where we already are following God and ignore "blindspots" or areas where we are not following God. Like the previous substitution, this substitution allows people to nod their head, say "Amen," and feel as if they are doing what the Bible says while avoiding the need to be more Christ-like in a different area of their lives. In contrast, the Bible authors repeatedly applauded their audiences for obedience while also challenging them to extend that same obedience to new fields in their reader's lives.[13]

Fifth, we substitute an emotional experience for a permanent behavioral change. People may feel emotional or convicted after hearing a sermon and leave believing God has spoken to them. But if people put their Bibles

---

11. Robinson, "The Heresy of Application."
12. Cf. Luke 6:46; John 14:15; Ephesians 4:1; James 2:17–19, 4:17.
13. Cf. Matthew 19:16–22; 2 Corinthians 8:7–8; Revelation 2:1–7, 12–17, 18–29.

Introduction

down after experiencing a feeling and do not live differently or follow God more closely, then they are substituting *feeling* God for *following* God.

Furthermore, some preachers act like application is accomplished simply because a passage has been explained. It is easy to assume listeners create applications for themselves simply because a text of Scripture has been put in front of them. Teachers and pastors forget that while we have pondered a passage for a full week, listeners are reading the text for the first time. Congregants thus cannot see the applications as readily as the well-prepared Bible teacher can. As a result, a preacher can feel as if his sermon has faithfully explained a text, yet faithful application never was made. This perhaps explains why some sermons sound more like dry commentaries rather than lively exhortations which drive the author's meaning home to audiences in meaningful, specific, and practical ways.

Why do we so often substitute other things for true application? This dilemma has not gone unnoticed by Christian scholars. As far back as the fourth century, the church father Augustine advised his readers on how to properly interpret and apply texts.[14] Unfortunately, some preaching works have propounded application only in the form of prohibitions. The preacher should not allegorize, spiritualize, or moralize.[15] Homiletical scholars often assume as long as the preacher avoids these prohibitions, then the sermon's applications inevitably will be text-grounded. On the other hand, other resources claim that the application will arise naturally if one discovers the original significance and somehow rewords that significance for today.[16] What is missing is the middle step: explaining how to keep authorial intent when moving from the past-tense of the text to the present world. None of the solutions above produce text-grounded applications on a consistent basis.

---

14. Cf. Augustine, *On Christian Doctrine*.

15. Allegorization happens when "instead of concentrating on the clear meaning, people relegate the text to merely reflecting another meaning beyond the text." Fee and Stuart, *How to Read the Bible for All Its Worth*, 91. Osborne says "Spiritualizing takes historical passages (such as the David and Jonathan story [1 Sam 20]) and uses it as a parable illustrating a spiritual reality (such as earthly friendship) . . . [ignoring] the intended theological meaning of the text." Osborne, *The Hermeneutical Spiral*, 442. Finally, Smith states, "Moralizing is when we reduce the message of an Old Testament narrative to whatever moral lesson can be gained. . . . The message of Christianity is not, 'Here are examples of how you can be a better person.' Rather, the message of Christianity is, 'You can never be better on your own. You need Christ.'" Smith, *Recapturing the Voice of God*, 54.

16. Stott, for example, only gives two steps to applying a text: "what did it mean when first spoken or written" and "how does it speak to us today?" Stott, *Between Two Worlds*, 221.

INTRODUCTION

Consequently, many scholars have agreed the needed middle step involves finding the theological principle the author intended to convey before making the leap to application.[17] However, while many authors agree theology can bridge exegesis with application, few have attempted to wed this concept to a genre-specific approach.[18] Walker comes closest to linking application to the genre of the text. He provides several characteristics of a text-grounded application based upon the author's intent to give a theological revelation about God and man.[19] He also gives one of the few analyses of how the genre of the text should be reflected in the sermon's application.[20] Unfortunately, he devotes only one page to elucidating this text-grounded application process.

A MODEL FOR GENRE-SPECIFIC EXPOSITORY APPLICATIONS

In summary, while much as been said about sermon applications and the use of theology to bridge to application, a gap still exists connecting the biblical genres to biblical application. Preachers need a positive model to demonstrate how to move from exegesis, to theological propositions, to practical applications while remaining sensitive to the genre of the text. This book argues that Alexander Maclaren provides such a model. Pace correctly argues, "By considering [Maclaren's] approach to relevant interpretation, preachers today can determine some practical guidelines for applying the timeless truths of Scripture for contemporary audiences."[21] Later he also adds, "The recognition of Maclaren's expositional skill combined with the relevant preaching acclaimed by the people of his day endorse Maclaren as an excellent example of how contemporary application may be made without violating the text's meaning."[22] Expository preachers still ought to study Maclaren in order to learn from his method of application.

---

17. E.g. Köstenberger and Patterson, *Invitation to Biblical Interpretation*, 790–94; Vines and Shaddix, *Power in the Pulpit*, 185; Kuruvilla, *Privilege the Text!*, 109–11.

18. E.g. Akin, "Applying a Text-Driven Sermon," 284; Black, "Exegesis for the Text-Driven Sermon," 152; Majors, "The Foundation for Text-Accurate Applications," 76–100.

19. Walker, *Let the Text Talk*, 64.

20. Walker, *Let the Text Talk*, 82.

21. Pace, "Alexander Maclaren," 71.

22. Pace, "Alexander Maclaren," 85.

Introduction

Powerful, text-grounded applications was a staple of his preaching and an emphasis of his study time. Maclaren said,

> The sermon's true purpose is to explain, confirm, and enforce Scripture. Once the text was followed by a sermon dealing with it. Would that it were [sic] always so now! Better to put new life into the old form by making a text really what it is mean to be, than to break through it in a flight after something 'fresh and unconventional.'[23]

Here is where Maclaren's sermons speak wisdom for contemporary preachers. They reveal a genre-specific process of application that can be a model for practical, text-driven applications. His sermons still speak today and deserve careful reading.

In order to "put new life into the old form," his sermon points roughly followed a common pattern. His applications were based, first of all, on solid exegesis of the text. His commitment to applying Scripture after a careful exegesis in the original language made him stand out from other preachers of his day.[24] Maclaren followed this teaching about the text by giving the theological lesson which the author hoped to convey. The theological lesson, or proposition, is the universal and timeless truth the biblical author purposed for his readers to learn. The biblical author's theological lesson is universally true regardless of time and culture. Finding the intended theological lesson of a text is vital because this lesson serves as the key to bridge the authorial intent with contemporary Christians. Since Maclaren consistently grounded his applications on the author's theological intent, his applications were text-grounded and specific. Therefore, his sermons can serve as a model for expository preachers today on how to preach the various genres of the Bible.

HOW THIS BOOK WILL MOVE FORWARD

Maclaren has over a thousand sermons in publication. However, his method of exposition has received little attention from scholarly resources. While Maclaren received much attention during and soon after his life, very little has been written on him recently. Therefore, the first chapter will trace the development of Maclaren's preaching practice and identify those factors which contributed to his growth as a preacher. By the time Maclaren came to Union Chapel in Manchester, he had already developed

23. Maclaren, "An Old Preacher on Preaching," 30.
24. Wilkinson, *Modern Masters of Pulpit Discourse*, 124.

Introduction

a preaching philosophy marked by evangelism, teaching, heralding, text-grounded application, and a commitment to keep Christ at the center of his preaching ministry. These qualities formed the foundation for his approach to preaching the different genres of the Bible.

Chapters two through six will dive into his sermons from the various biblical genres. Here is where the sermons of Maclaren speak wisdom for contemporary preachers. Each chapter begins with an overview of the respective genre followed by steps for how to model Maclaren's method of preaching. In essence, these chapters take his sermons and ask the question, "If Maclaren were alive today, what would he say to preachers about how to apply the genres of the Bible?" The conclusions are based upon his sermons and can be read as the voice of Maclaren for today. In this sense, Maclaren still speaks, and Bible expositors would be wise to listen intently to this prince of expositors. Each chapter then will summarize the major practices text-driven preachers can take away from Maclaren. A breakdown of one sermon and discussion questions for further reflection will conclude the chapters.

Chapter eight will summarize the book as a whole. Alexander Maclaren can serve as a model for text-appropriate and genre-specific applications. His expertise in exegesis made him uniquely suited for preaching the whole Bible. Across Scripture, Maclaren's faithfulness to exegesis helped him identify the universal, theological principle of a passage before applying it to his congregation. Are you ready to see Maclaren's process in action? First, let us be introduced to Maclaren the man and find what personal influences and preaching practices produced one of the greatest expository preachers in Christian history.

DISCUSSION QUESTIONS

1. Why do you think we sometimes struggle to apply the Bible personal and practically to our individual lives and communities? What are some things we often do instead of thinking of personal and practical applications?

2. In what ways can we allow observing and interpreting the text to take the place of making practical and personal applications?

3. Why is applying the Bible a necessary part of the Bible study and teaching process? What do people miss out if text-grounded applications are skipped?

1

Life Lessons and Preaching Practices

"It is quite true that the Gospel is simple, but it is also true that it is deep, and they will best appreciate its simplicity who have most honestly endeavoured to fathom its depth."

—ALEXANDER MACLAREN

ONE NEWSPAPER EDITOR DESCRIBED what it was like to listen to Alexander Maclaren preach to his congregation at Union Chapel in Manchester, England:

> He stands preaching, flushed now and warmed, every fibre braced, every gesture alive, his voice ringing vibrant; and quite surely one knows that here, at last, is the true preacher—a man preaching from himself. . . . There is no flights of oratory, no tricks of style or manner, no displays of learning, no flowery digressions; . . . not even the power of thought, or humour, or emotions; not this or that holds captive, but the plain conviction of the man. . . . 'There you sit, my brother,' he seems to say—to me only amid the multitude.[1]

Ever since his time at Union Chapel, Maclaren has been called the prince of expositors. In fact, following the death of Charles Spurgeon in 1892,

---

1. Williamson, *Life of Alexander Maclaren*, 126–27.

Maclaren was considered to be the best living preacher in the world. So what did he do that contributed to this preaching prowess? That answer cannot be fully discovered without first understanding his homiletical philosophy and the people that influenced him. As Pace correctly notes, "The collective influence of his education, his family, and mentoring ministers culminated to produce a preacher whose 'theological position was candidly and thoughtfully evangelical.'"[2] This chapter will summarize the lessons preachers and teachers can learn from Maclaren's life and preaching practices.

THE LIFE OF ALEXANDER MACLAREN

Maclaren was born in Glasgow, Scotland, on February 11, 1826.[3] He was the youngest of six children in a family of very devoted Christians.[4] His mother, Mary Wingate, was known for being intelligent, patient, calm, wise, and loving. His father, David Maclaren, was a city merchant and gifted lay preacher. David Maclaren's devotion to preaching made a lasting impression on young Alexander. Writing in the third person, he said, "The writer was too young to form a judgment of his father's sermons, but not too young to receive an impression which has powerfully influenced him in his own work, and abides with him still."[5]

---

2. Pace, "Alexander Maclaren," 72–73, citing Dargan, *History of Preaching*, 573.

3. McLaren, *Dr. McLaren of Manchester*, 5. E. T. MacLaren was Alexander's cousin and sister-in-law. Larsen, *Company of Preachers*, 582. Maclaren would sign his name "McLaren" but publish his books as "Maclaren." He changed it because he thought the Highland Scottish version of the name looked ugly when printed. McLaren, *Dr. McLaren of Manchester*, iv, 27–28. Maclaren said once, "All my people, and I think all my 'clan,' go in for the Mc, and I use it always, except on title-pages. I took to the other in my first volume, partly because Macmillan, the publisher . . . whose clan always go for the 'Mac,' wished it, and partly because it looks better on a title-page. But, as you perhaps have never observed, I sign McL. My brother-in-law is deeply grieved at my defection; but it is a mere matter of spelling, and I decided it on aesthetic grounds." Williamson, *Life of Alexander Maclaren*, 219. Wilkinson, the author of *Modern Masters of Pulpit Discourse*, noted that in his correspondence with MacLaren, he signed with the Scottish Mc and an upper case "L," such as "McLaren." Sometimes he would put a dot under the *c* to indicate the abbreviation. Wilkinson, *Modern Masters of Pulpit Discourse*, 115.

4. McLaren, *Dr. McLaren of Manchester*, 19; cf. Williamson, *Life of Alexander Maclaren*, 18.

5. McLaren, *Dr. McLaren of Manchester*, 3.

Life Lessons and Preaching Practices

The greatest legacy David left for Alexander was his passion for God's Word and the careful exposition of Scripture. Scottish Baptist preachers like David Maclaren tended to be bi-vocational but "keen students of the Scriptures."[6] David's preaching was known for being expository, intellectually stimulating, and evangelistic. He studied the Scriptures carefully before preaching, then delivered his sermon with passionate power.[7] He also argued that ministers should be educated and trained, so he advocated starting a Baptist theological school in Scotland.[8] David's son, Alexander, echoed these same passions in his preaching philosophy.

Alexander Maclaren was very intelligent but shy, and he sought to pass time by himself.[9] He learned to read early in life and enjoyed reading by himself rather than joining in on children's games. His oldest sister said that Maclaren's worst fits as a child occurred every time his mother wanted him to attend children's parties. Though once he was forced to interact, he could be very friendly.[10] This character trait stuck with him for his whole life.[11] He attended Glasgow High School and received many "prizes" in high school. The master of the school once remarked to the provost, "This young gentleman has to appear before us so often that he had better be accommodated with a seat nearer the table."[12] High school taught Maclaren his study and work habits. He would later apply these habits to the study of Scripture in the original languages.[13]

Maclaren recalled enjoying church services and family devotions every Sunday.[14] He also attended a Bible class taught by the Congregational minister David Russell. Russell was a source of spiritual counsel for Maclaren at a young age. He learned from Russell how to have a living faith that is surrendered to God and for God's glory. Maclaren later said of Russell, "To him, under God, I owe the quickening of early religious impressions into living faith and surrender, and to him I owe also much wise and affectionate

---

6. Carlile, *Alexander Maclaren, D.D.*, 14.
7. Williamson, *Life of Alexander Maclaren*, 6, 9, 15.
8. Little, "Historical Registers of Scottish Baptists," 231.
9. Meyer, "Alexander Maclaren: An Appreciation," 9.
10. McLaren, *Dr. McLaren of Manchester*, 2, 8.
11. Meyer, "Alexander Maclaren," 14.
12. McLaren, *Dr. McLaren of Manchester*, 11–12.
13. Carlile, *Alexander Maclaren, D.D.*, 15.
14. McLaren, *Dr. McLaren of Manchester*, 8–9.

counsel in my boyish years."[15] It was through Russell and the Bible class that Maclaren became saved and followed a call into the ministry.

Maclaren was eager to join the church after salvation, even at fourteen years old, and was baptized on May 17, 1840, by James Patterson in Hope Street Baptist Church. Maclaren could not recall discussing his calling to ministry with his parents. However, as he became older, several people noted his intellectual prowess and potential for future pastoral ministry. Maclaren claimed he and his family always knew God had called him into the ministry.[16] David Maclaren even took his son to a family friend, Rev. Charles Stovel, one day to ask if he thought Alexander would make a good preacher. "Mr. Stovel, after due consideration said, 'Well, Well, perhaps he might.'"[17]

David Maclaren moved his family to London so that his son could attend Stepney College.[18] Maclaren barely passed the admissions interview but was accepted in 1842 despite being only sixteen. Most of the admissions committee were skeptical. However, one member of the admissions committee, Samuel Green, went home and told his family that "the Committee had passed a Scotch lad named Maclaren, who would cut all the others out."[19] Carlile states of those years,

> The toil at Stepney laid the foundation of all that superstructure raised in after years. Books were food to him. The range of his reading was very wide in philosophy and travels and Christian authors, but he is mainly a "man of one book." The Bible was not only his text book, but his constant companion: he knows it as a doctor knows his *Materia Medica*, and in this he stands out as an example to all students.[20]

His time at Stepney College built the foundation upon which Maclaren developed his homiletical practice.

The school hired a new principal in 1844 named Benjamin Davies. Davies instilled in Maclaren a high view of God's majesty, the universal

---

15. Nicoll, *Princes of the Church*, 244.
16. McLaren, *Dr. McLaren of Manchester*, 18–19.
17. Carlile, *Alexander Maclaren, D.D.*, 18.
18. McLaren, *Dr. McLaren of Manchester*, 3, 20.
19. Carlile, *Alexander Maclaren, D.D.*, 18. Cf. Williamson, *Life of Alexander Maclaren*, 20.
20. Carlile, *Alexander Maclaren, D.D.*, 35.

Life Lessons and Preaching Practices

corruption of sin, and a love for the Hebrew language.[21] More importantly, he learned from Davies the importance of basing a sermon on careful exegesis of a text in the original language.[22] Carlile describes Davies this way: "He was as painstaking and as scientific in examining a Hebrew word as a physician over the scrutinizing of a cell in which some foreign element appeared that might mean life or death to the patient."[23] Maclaren's commitment to carefully exegete a text in the original languages can be traced back to Davies.

Davies was not the only man during this time to make a major impact on Maclaren's ministry. Thomas Binney was his primary homiletical influence, as he later recounted: "It was Binney who taught me to preach."[24] Binney was the pastor of King's Weigh-House Chapel in London.[25] He was known for being very articulate, having a strong grasp of the English language, preaching with enthusiasm and force, delivering heart-to-heart appeals, and using no notes or manuscript in the pulpit.[26] Maclaren often went to hear him preach on Sundays and took from Binney the practice of preaching without notes, deriving sermon divisions from the text's divisions, and carefully communicating the message from the Bible.[27]

Maclaren's first preaching opportunity came with his trial sermon before a college committee of six teachers. Their conclusion was a simple "he would do." His first opportunity before a congregation was in the college's old chapel on a Sunday afternoon when he was seventeen years old. Only seven individuals were in attendance at that service.[28] Then, on one of his trips back to Edinburgh, a local Baptist church asked him to preach. His family heard about it, and several distant members and cousins came to hear him. He later recounted about that day, "It was cruel, McLaren eyes everywhere."[29]

---

21. Sellers, "Other Times, Other Ministries," 191; Stewart, "Dr. Alexander Maclaren," 35.

22. Maclaren, *Best of Alexander MacLaren*, 9.

23. Carlile, *Alexander Maclaren, D.D.*, 21.

24. McLaren, *Dr. McLaren of Manchester*, 48.

25. Larsen, *Company of Preachers*, vol. 2, 452–53.

26. Larsen, *Company of Preachers*, vol. 2, 452–53; Webber, *History of Preaching in Britain and America*, 480–81.

27. Pace, "Alexander Maclaren," 72.

28. Carlile, *Alexander Maclaren, D.D.*, 24–25; Williamson, *Life of Alexander Maclaren*, 3.

29. McLaren, *Dr. McLaren of Manchester*, 26.

For most of his college years, Maclaren flew under the radar. He was best remembered in college as a student who was a hard worker and loved studying. He did eventually receive several prizes for his academic work, including a first prize in the category of "Theological Honours."[30]

With one year left until graduation, the Stepney College administration asked him to preach at Portland Chapel in Southampton on November 14, 1845.[31] The church liked him and invited him to fill the pulpit for the next three months. At the end of that time, they invited him to be their pastor after he graduated the next year. Portland Chapel in Southampton could hold several hundred people, but at the time it had two hundred members and only fifty consistently in Sunday attendance. Maclaren blamed this on the unwise conduct of his predecessors. The church had a checkered past with constant pastoral turnover; the previous two pastors served only three years and two years. They both left due to their inability to cope with the difficulty of caring for and growing the church. Consequently, the church had a negative reputation in the community. It was £200 in debt and needed £60 worth of repairs. However, they offered Maclaren £60 a year in faith, not knowing if they would be able to pay it.[32] He was shocked they asked him to fill such a responsibility, and he felt unfit for the task. After consulting with his father, who advised him to take the position, he accepted the call to Portland Chapel. In a letter he wrote, "It is this which I like about the place that if the worst comes to the worst I shall at all events not have to reflect that I have killed a flourishing plant but only assisted at the funeral of a withered one."[33]

Portland Chapel afforded him the opportunity to test, practice, and perfect his preaching method. He resolved to study diligently for every sermon.[34] He became fluent in Greek, Hebrew, and German and began translating a chapter in the Bible from the Hebrew and in Greek everyday.[35] Yet even in all his labor in preaching, Maclaren understood that God ultimately is the source of power. He wrote in a letter after leaving Southampton:

---

30. Williamson, *Life of Alexander Maclaren*, 25; Patrick, "Prince of Preachers," 7.

31. Wimberly, *Modern Apostles of Faith*, 91.

32. McLaren, *Dr. McLaren of Manchester*, 29–39; Carlile, *Alexander Maclaren, D.D.*, 47–48; Wiersbe, *50 People*, 108.

33. McLaren, *Dr. McLaren of Manchester*, 31.

34. McLaren, *Dr. McLaren of Manchester*, 38.

35. Williamson, *Life of Alexander Maclaren*, 33.

Life Lessons and Preaching Practices

I have learned, I shall never unlearn, lessons that after all, our sole power lies in the true, simple, sincere setting forth the living Christ, and I have adjured for evermore all the rubbish of 'intellectual preaching.' I would rather serve out slops for people to live upon than lumps of stone cut into the form of loaves.[36]

For the rest of his life, Maclaren would emphasize hard work coupled with personal devotion to Christ.

Maclaren's years at Portland Chapel were not without controversy. Some members of the church thought his manner and preaching were too radical and not orthodox enough. For example, he discarded parts of the traditional ministerial uniform like the white tie.[37] He also was more gifted as a preacher than a pastor, not spending much time in visitation or social gatherings but in studying and teaching.[38] He did not view preaching as a greater responsibility than other pastoral duties but felt that preaching was God's special calling for him. All his mind and effort was put into developing his sermons.[39] His critics were dramatically reduced when the church began to grow.[40]

While Maclaren did not go on many pastoral calls, he did enjoy educating young adults. He took advantage of offers to speak on literature, history, and the relationship between church and state at the local athenaeum.[41] Outside of these lectures, however, he shied away from the public eye. He frequently declined invitations to preach at other churches on Sundays and to deliver lectures during the week, even if the invitation came from a city more prominent than Southampton. He reasoned that God had called him to Portland Chapel, so he needed to minister to his congregation.[42] After his marriage, though, his wife Marion regarded such invitations as a duty he owed. She convinced him not to refuse all of them.[43]

Maclaren called his time at Portland Chapel a "long hard discouraging work," but he saw great fruit.[44] He quickly gained a reputation for bold

---

36. McLaren, *Dr. McLaren of Manchester*, 62.
37. Sellers, "Other Times, Other Ministries," 189; Carlile, *Alexander Maclaren, D.D.*, 49.
38. McLaren, *Dr. McLaren of Manchester*, 48–49, 75.
39. Currier, *Nine Great Preachers*, 288. Cf. Patrick, "Prince of Preachers," 7.
40. Webber, *Preaching in Britain and America*, 572.
41. McLaren, *Dr. McLaren of Manchester*, 57; Carlile, *Alexander Maclaren, D.D.*, 57.
42. Williamson, *Life of Alexander Maclaren*, 23.
43. McLaren, *Dr. McLaren of Manchester*, 57–58.
44. McLaren, *Dr. McLaren of Manchester*, 43.

preaching. His first sermons were short, lasting fifteen or twenty minutes, and he had long pauses where he searched for the perfect word. This was perhaps due to his decision early in his ministry to preach without notes.[45] Maclaren later denounced such claims of short sermons and long pauses as "legendary."[46] These stressors, combined with his natural shyness, resulted in severe stage fright. He struggled to control his nerves his whole ministry career.[47]

The church grew, paid off its debts, repaired its facilities, and improved its reputation in the community.[48] His success at Portland Chapel was soon becoming well-known outside of Southhampton, and in 1858, Union Chapel in Manchester found themselves in need of a pastor. They had heard of the budding young preacher and extended an invitation to Maclaren to fill their pulpit one Sunday. Knowing they might ask him to become their pastor, he hesitantly preached at the church in April. Union Chapel decided to reach out to him the very next day about the pastoral position. Although he was hesitant to move from the rural environment of Southampton, God was leading him to accept the position because he could impact more people for God's Kingdom in Manchester. He reluctantly accepted the call and preached his last sermon as Portland Chapel's pastor on June 20, 1858.[49] The people were saddened by the news, but they agreed with him that he could do more for God's kingdom in Manchester than in Southampton.[50] He was forever thankful for the lessons learned at Portland Chapel, as he told a group of pastors:

> I thank God ... that I was stuck down in a quiet little obscure place to begin my ministry, for that is what spoils half of you young fellows, you get pitchforked into prominent positions at once, and then fritter yourselves away in all manner of little engagements that you call duties, going to this tea-meeting, and that anniversary and other breakfast celebration, instead of stopping at home and reading your Bibles and getting near to God. I thank God for the early days of struggle and obscurity.[51]

---

45. Brown, *Puritan Preaching in England*, 268.
46. McLaren, *Dr. McLaren of Manchester*, 36.
47. Carlile, *Alexander Maclaren, D.D.*, 51.
48. Carlile, *Alexander Maclaren, D.D.*, 50; Wiersbe, *50 People*, 108.
49. McLaren, *Dr. McLaren of Manchester*, 59.
50. Carlile, *Alexander Maclaren, D.D.*, 55.
51. Carlile, *Alexander Maclaren, D.D.*, 51.

Life Lessons and Preaching Practices

Thus, at Portland Chapel, Maclaren built upon the foundation laid in his childhood and collegiate years. The skills and lessons learned there would catapult Maclaren into becoming the most popular expositor in Victorian England.

Maclaren began his pastorate at Union Chapel in July of 1858. He was thirty-two years old.[52] In 1858, Union Chapel was considered the second most affluent church in Manchester.[53] It had a membership role of about 240, but the church began to see growth soon after Maclaren's arrival.[54] By 1862 the church had more than doubled in attendance.[55] The building filled so quickly that some people attempted to bribe the doormen with the hopes of getting better seats.[56] In addition to his Sunday sermons, Maclaren preached a Bible lesson on Wednesday nights. These were attended by many from across the city, and some argued that they were better than his Sunday morning sermons because they had more exegetical depth.[57] His first sermons to be printed came in the second year of his pastorate, *Sermons Preached in Manchester, First Series*.[58] Nicoll states that this book had to be "simply dragged out of him" and that "if he had been left to himself he would never have published any sermons."[59]

Soon the original church building could not support the growth. So, in 1869, the church bought land in the suburbs near Whitworth Park to build a larger sanctuary. Maclaren was reluctant to build a larger sanctuary because he did not believe that more people would desire to hear him preach.[60] The new building was opened on November 16, 1869.[61] It sat 1400, but more chairs could be added bringing the maximum capacity close to 2000.[62] The new church building also contained a lecture hall

---

52. McLaren, *Dr. McLaren of Manchester*, 58–59, 67.

53. Sellers, "Other Times, Other Ministries," 192.

54. Sellers, "Other Times, Other Ministries," 192.

55. Williamson, *Life of Alexander Maclaren*, 40.

56. Hamer, "Dr. McLaren and Union Chapel," 36.

57. Hamer, "Dr. McLaren and Union Chapel," 35; Carlile, *Alexander Maclaren, D.D.*, 89.

58. Maclaren, *Sermons Preached in Manchester: First Series*.

59. Nicoll, *Princes of the Church*, 253.

60. McLaren, *Dr. McLaren of Manchester*, 104.

61. Hamer, "Dr. McLaren and Union Chapel," 31; Carlile, *Alexander Maclaren, D.D.*, 88.

62. Hughes, "Union Chapel, Manchester," 93; Hamer, "Dr. McLaren and Union Chapel," 31.

with 500 used for weeknight services. The building was designed in the Gothic style and garnered the title of the Baptist Cathedral of Lancashire or the Nonconformist Cathedral of Lancashire.[63] Maclaren's doubts about the move proved unwarranted. Even after building a larger sanctuary, people were soon forced to sit next to and even behind the pulpit.[64] Union Chapel continued to grow, and in 1880 even more classrooms were added.[65]

As in his time at Portland Chapel, Maclaren rarely accepted calls to preach outside Union Chapel on Sundays unless it was with smaller Baptist church or a village chapel.[66] However, he did become involved in wider denominational work. He was a regular preacher and special guest for events throughout the city. He also befriended, advised, and mentored other preachers in the city and surrounding area.[67] Furthermore, his published sermons were becoming popular reading by 1875. Every week, a stenographer recorded the Sunday sermon and gave Maclaren the manuscript. He would make a few small changes to the manuscript then send it to the *Baptist Times* for publication.[68] The reason few changes were made was that he spoke in near-perfect English.[69]

By the end of 1875, Maclaren's method and style of preaching were fully developed. He was now a well-known preacher, which helped him get elected as the president of the Baptist Union of Great Britain in 1875. At forty-nine, he was the youngest person to hold the office up to that time.[70] As part of his presidential duties, he shared the preaching platform with other Baptist elites including Charles H. Spurgeon.

Maclaren and Spurgeon knew each other well and had a friendship built upon mutual respect. Maclaren spoke highly of Spurgeon as both a biblical scholar and homiletician.[71] Spurgeon likewise said that Maclaren was "a tower of strength to the evangelical faith."[72] Carlile described their relationship this way:

63. Hughes, "Union Chapel, Manchester," 93; Carlile, *Alexander Maclaren, D.D.*, 88.
64. Calkins, *Master Preachers*, 37.
65. Hamer, "Dr. McLaren and Union Chapel," 31.
66. Wiersbe, *50 People*, 111.
67. McLaren, *Dr. McLaren of Manchester*, 110.
68. Williamson, *Life of Alexander Maclaren*, 94–95.
69. Maclaren, *Best of Alexander MacLaren*, 17.
70. Carlile, *Alexander Maclaren, D.D.*, 110–21; Currier, *Nine Great Preachers*, 307.
71. Wilkinson, *Modern Masters of Pulpit Discourse*, 116.
72. Pattison, *History of Christian Preaching*, 341.

> There is hardly any comparison possible between Spurgeon and Maclaren, except that they preached the same Gospel. They belong to different types. Their friendship was long and loyal. When the unhappy "Down-grade" controversy split the ranks of the Baptist denomination to an extent that will require a generation to heal, these men had no words of bitterness for each other, only regret that they were not on the same platform.[73]

The Down-grade controversy occurred in 1887 when Spurgeon published several articles in his *Sword and Trowel* stating his concerns over liberal theology growing in the Baptist Union.[74] Maclaren was one of four representatives the Baptist Union sent to meet with Spurgeon over the matter. He originally was chosen to be one of the four representatives because the Baptist Union knew Spurgeon considered him to be a good-standing Baptist. Unlike Spurgeon, Maclaren was more open to the Baptist Union accepting wider theological beliefs; nevertheless, he sought for peaceful reconciliation and did not want the Baptist Union to attack Spurgeon. He wanted Spurgeon to stay in the Baptist Union and for the Union to concede to some of Spurgeon's demands.[75] Maclaren was the only representative of the four that took such an approach with Spurgeon. Maclaren was eventually left out of exchanges among the other three representatives.[76]

Despite Maclaren's efforts, Spurgeon left the Baptist Union.[77] Thankfully, this did not sever their friendship. When Spurgeon died, Maclaren was one of the speakers at his memoriam service.[78] Later in his life, Maclaren read Spurgeon's sermons devotionally and said he had "been wonderfully helped and stirred by them. There is a passion of love to Jesus, and a grand fullness of trust in Him which have stirred and rebuked me."[79] He also presided over the ceremony for the unveiling of Spurgeon's statue at the Baptist Church House. He said of Spurgeon at this ceremony, "He was in the true succession of Latimer and Luther and John Bunyan. . . . We all of

---

73. Carlile, *Alexander Maclaren, D.D.*, 118.
74. Wiersbe, *Walking with the Giants*, 74.
75. Hopkins, "Down-Grade Controversy," 339.
76. Hopkins, "Down-Grade Controversy," 264–69.
77. Larsen, *Company of Preachers*, 582.
78. Carlile, *Alexander Maclaren, D.D.*, 137.
79. McLaren, *Dr. McLaren of Manchester*, 244–45.

us bow down to him with the recognition of that preeminence of spiritual and homiletical power."[80]

In 1877 the University of Edinburgh conferred upon Maclaren a Doctor of Divinity degree. As a Baptist, he was the first Nonconformist, non-Presbyterian to receive that honor.[81] He also was continually asked by Robert Dale to deliver the Lyman Beecher Yale lectures in America, which he declined because he did not want the publicity.[82]

Despite Maclaren's fame, the great emotional and mental strain he felt when preaching started to take a toll. Frequent bouts with sickness and feebleness culminated with a severe illness in 1881 that required him to take a year-long vacation. It left him permanently weakened. He suffered during this time with depression and thoughts of resignation.[83] Union Chapel decided to hire an associate pastor so Maclaren could do less pastoral care and administrative duties. His preaching schedule was also reduced to once on Sunday and once on Wednesday.[84]

Then, in 1884, he faced his darkest hour. His wife Marion of twenty-eight years died on December 21 after fighting an illness for eleven days.[85] While the loss of a spouse is always difficult, it was particularly so for Maclaren who saw Marion as his greatest influence and source of emotional strength. She was his sweetheart since childhood.[86] They were married on March 27, 1856, and she made their home a joy.[87] She was well-educated, a natural leader, intelligent, and humorous. She also was more sociable and outgoing compared to Maclaren. He praised her for being a loving and unselfish wife.[88]

Marion had made an immensely positive impact on Maclaren's ministry.[89] E. T. McLaren, Alexander's cousin, witnessed her influence first hand. According to E. T. McLaren, Marion encouraged her husband, worked

80. Williamson, *Life of Alexander Maclaren*, 227–28.
81. Stewart, "Dr. Alexander Maclaren," 41; Carlile, *Alexander Maclaren, D.D.*, 88–89.
82. Williamson, *Life of Alexander Maclaren*, 82.
83. McLaren, *Dr. McLaren of Manchester*, 117.
84. Carlile, *Alexander Maclaren, D.D.*, 92; McLaren, *Dr. McLaren of Manchester*, 144–45.
85. Currier, *Nine Great Preachers*, 307.
86. Wimberly, *Modern Apostles of Faith*, 91.
87. Carlile, *Alexander Maclaren, D.D.*, 54.
88. McLaren, *Dr. McLaren of Manchester*, 52–55.
89. Stewart, "Dr. Alexander Maclaren," 36; Williamson, *Life of Alexander Maclaren*, 32; Currier, *Nine Great Preachers*, 306.

Life Lessons and Preaching Practices

to shelter him from unnecessary cares and fears, helped him combat his stage fright, and prompted him to accept preaching engagements outside his church. In 1877, Maclaren published his weekday lessons as *Weekday Evening Addresses* because Marion urged him to do so.[90] Furthermore, for years he wanted to preach through a book of the Bible but feared his church would not like it. Finally, he preached Colossians only because Marion encouraged him to do it. These sermons later formed the basis of his volume in *Expositor's Bible*.[91] Maclaren himself said his wife was the primary influencer of his life. The *British Monthly* published a brief sketch of his life in 1905. He said the article missed "two regrettable gaps," the most important of which was his wife's influence on his work. He said of his wife,

> It should be told that the best part of it all came and comes from her. We read and thought together, and her clear, bright intellect illumined obscurities and 'rejoiced in the truth.' We worked and bore together, and her courage and deftness made toil easy and charmed away difficulties. She lived a life of nobleness, of strenuous effort, of aspiration, of sympathy, self-forgetfulness, and love. She was my guide, my inspirer, my corrector, my reward. Of all human formative influences on my character and life hers is the strongest and the best. To write of me and not to name her is to present a fragment.[92]

From Maclaren's own perspective, his wife Marion perhaps made a greater impact on Maclaren's ministry than any other individual following his years at Portland Chapel.

Maclaren never completely recovered from Marion's death, and some who knew him thought he would never preach again.[93] Soon afterwards, his health began to decline even more. As a result, he became increasingly focused on his preaching, publishing ministry, and denomination work, leaving his associate pastor to other duties at Union Chapel. He declined an invitation to become the Professor of Hebrew at the Baptist College at Regent's Park as well as the pastor of the church there called Bloomsbury Chapel.[94] He also received several calls to become the pastor of other

---

90. Maclaren, *Week-Day Evening Addresses*.

91. McLaren, *Dr. McLaren of Manchester*, 120–21 and 223–25; Maclaren, *Epistles to Colossians and Philemon*.

92. Nicoll, *Princes of the Church*, 244.

93. Maclaren, *Best of Alexander MacLaren*, 14.

94. Carlile, *Alexander Maclaren, D.D.*, 90.

churches, but Maclaren disliked change, which reinforced his desire to stay at Union Chapel.[95] Most of his published volumes come from the last part of his life as well. In 1896, he was recognized as one of the chief literary influences in Manchester by the principal of Owens College.[96] In 1902 he was given an honorary Doctor of Letters degree by the University of Manchester, elected Governor of the University of Manchester, established the University of Manchester's theological faculty, and became president of the Baptist Union for a second time.[97] By this time in his career, he was considered "the most distinguished Baptist preacher living."[98] He later received another Doctor of Divinity degree from the University of Glasgow.[99]

Maclaren was extended an invitation to speak at the Joint Assembly of the Baptist and Congregational Unions on April 23, 1901. He accepted, and it was at this historic conference Maclaren spoke his famous lecture describing the office of preacher titled "An Old Preacher on Preaching." Not long after the conference, though, Maclaren's health worsened once again, and his doctor ordered him to limit his speaking engagements outside of Manchester if he wanted to continue preaching every Sunday at Union Chapel.[100] He faced several months of poor health and eventually came to the conclusion that the time had come for him to retire from Union Chapel. His final sermon as the pastor of Union Chapel was on June 28, 1903.[101] For the remainder of his life, Maclaren lived in Scotland and only accepted invitations to preach in front of small, rural churches.

Dr. William Robertson Nicoll approached Maclaren about publishing a series of his sermons in the order of their biblical text as a resource called *Expositions of Holy Scripture*. Maclaren then showed Nicoll his preaching files. Beginning in Southampton in 1846, Maclaren had kept the outlines of every sermon he had preached, arranged in order of their biblical text. Under Nicoll's insistence, Maclaren went to work creating his magnum opus. He selected, edited, and filled out the sermon notes using a stenographer.

---

95. Williamson, *Life of Alexander Maclaren*, 44.

96. Hamer, "Dr. McLaren and Union Chapel," 34.

97. McLaren, *Dr. McLaren of Manchester*, 177–78; Carlile, *Alexander Maclaren, D.D.*, 138.

98. Williamson, *Life of Alexander Maclaren*, 123.

99. McLaren, *Dr. McLaren of Manchester*, 115.

100. Williamson, *Life of Alexander Maclaren*, 157–58.

101. McLaren, *Dr. McLaren of Manchester*, 198–204; Williamson, *Life of Alexander Maclaren*, 181–91, 244–45.

He also submitted several new sermons to the series. Nicoll added other sermons and Bible study lessons which had been previously published. Editing his *Expositions* became Maclaren's focus until the end of his life. His stenographer reported that on several occasions Maclaren looked at an outline and said, "'I can make nothing of it.' But very often this declaration was followed by a sudden change. He seemed all at once to take fire. I had to write as fast as possible, and even then I felt that I had to make him wait unduly."[102]

The last major event in Maclaren's life came in 1905 when he was elected the first president of the Baptist World Congress.[103] Afterwards, he remained in isolation in Scotland until he passed away on May 5, 1910, at 3:15 p.m. in his home at Whitehouse Terrace in Edinburgh. He was cremated and his ashes were placed in a grave in Brooklands Cemetery, where his wife and one daughter were buried.[104]

While pastors can glean much wisdom from Maclaren's life, it perhaps can best be summed up with the word "faithfulness." He was faithful to Christ. He was faithful to his wife. He was faithful to the churches where he was called. He faithfully studied and exposited God's Word. Finally, he was faithful to make preaching a primary focus of his ministry. While his life certainly can lead pastors to many life lessons, his faithfulness in everything he did stands out as a chief quality of his life.

MACLAREN'S PREACHING PRACTICES

Alexander Maclaren's early life and career molded him into a preacher who held one of the most prominent pulpits in Victorian England. This raises the question: what characteristics of his preaching contributed to this pulpit prowess? Maclaren himself had a few theories related to his sermon effectiveness.[105]

One day, Maclaren was asked to describe what a preacher does. In this lecture, which was titled "An Old Preacher on Preaching," Maclaren stated that a preacher is a combination of three biblical offices: evangelist, teacher, and prophet:

102. McLaren, *Dr. McLaren of Manchester*, 234–35, 249, 254.
103. McLaren, *Dr. McLaren of Manchester*, 204, 239.
104. Williamson, *Life of Alexander Maclaren*, 250–58.
105. Some portions of this section have been adapted from Mills, "Great Preachers and Their Preaching: Alexander Maclaren."

> The three-fold beam may be separated into its parts by a prism, but neither of these three is sunshine. The preacher has to try to re-combine them into the sweet, all-blessing white ray, which every eye feels to be light. We are preachers—that is to say, we are Evangelists, Teachers, Prophets. Let us not limit ourselves to either function, but try always to blend the three in that one which should include them all.[106]

As an evangelist, the preacher delivers good news to sinful souls, preaches the crucifixion of Christ, shows the universal reality of sin and only deliverance in Christ, speaks in a clear manner, uses urgency, displays personal tender care, and is willing to change methods to reach people.[107] Since the preacher is an evangelist, the sermon should be Christ-centered. He elaborated,

> "Nothing odd lasts," but Christ lasts, and man's sins last, and man's need lasts, and we have got to preach Christ and Him crucified, the Saviour of mankind. And I have tried to preach Christ as if I believe in Him, not as if I had hesitations and peradventures and limitations, and I have tried to preach Him as if I lived on Him, and that is the bottom of it all, that we shall ourselves feed on the truth that we proclaim to others, so if my words can reach any of my dear younger brethren this morning I do want to say, concentrate yourself on the work of your ministry, preach the Bible and its truth, preach Christ the Redeemer, preach Him with all your heart, lift up your voice, lift it up with strength, be not afraid. We know that the Son of God has come: and He has given us an understanding that we may know Him that is true, even in His Son Jesus Christ. Brethren, depend on it that if these be the themes and that be the spirit of our ministry, whether they will bear, or whether they will forbear, they will know that there has been a prophet among them.[108]

Elsewhere Maclaren spoke powerfully about the importance of the gospel in the sermon:

> Brethren! preach [sic] *Him*—preach His Cross. It will find an echo in men's hearts. It will appeal to a deeper stratum of their being than any arguments of ours can penetrate. It carries its own best evidence with it. It puts forth its own might when it is presented in its own

---

106. Maclaren, "Old Preacher on Preaching," 38.
107. Maclaren, "Old Preacher on Preaching," 21–25.
108. Carlile, *Alexander Maclaren, D.D.*, 108.

> simplicity. Let us preach it lovingly, pleadingly, authoritatively—as fact, as a truth, as the power of God; and be sure that whatever weakness there may be in us, however we may feel incompetent to deal with the difficulties of this generation, He will be with us, and will fulfill His own word: "I, if I be lifted up on the Cross, will draw all men unto Me." Yes, even though it be held but by our feeble hands, trembling, stained, unworthy. Yes. He, not we; His power, not our genius, or eloquence, or argumentation; His Gospel, not our preaching, will draw hearts to Himself, there to be at rest.[109]

Maclaren sought to fulfill the role of the evangelist whenever he preached, believing Christ was the only solution to the problems and questions of the world.

Maclaren also saw the preacher as a teacher. Teaching is necessary because conversion and sanctification come through hearing the truths of God's Word alone. Therefore, sermons, centered on the Bible, are sufficient to address any need. Since only Scripture transforms people, Maclaren argued that teaching should be an exposition of Scripture and not an opinion on current events.[110] He said,

> We sometimes hear it said, Preach Christ and not doctrines; and with certain limitations and explanations the advice may be good; but the antithesis is false and misleading. For what, in the name of common sense, is a Christ without "doctrines" about Him? A sound, and nothing more; six letters of unmeaning word, as empty as any name in the genealogies of the Book of Chronicles. What possible way is there of knowing a person whom one has never seen, but by teachings concerning his acts and character? . . . The history becomes a Gospel by the presence of the doctrine—as touching his Person that He is the Son of God, as touching his Death that it is the sacrifice for the sins of the world.[111]

The office of teacher required the preacher to work hard to study the Bible and to improve his preaching skills so he could disseminate, or spread, the truths of Scripture more clearly.[112] Like a teacher, the preacher's ultimate goal is to build up his hearers' knowledge and skills so that they can draw near to God for themselves without the help of the teacher.[113] The teaching

---

109. Maclaren, "Gospel for the Day," 27–28. Emphasis original.
110. Maclaren, "Old Preacher on Preaching," 25–33.
111. Maclaren, "Gospel for the Day," 8–9.
112. Maclaren, "Counsels for the Study and the Life," 168.
113. Maclaren, *Secret of Power*, 258.

aspect of preaching had a direct relationship to Maclaren's commitment to expository preaching and to text-warranted applications.

While Maclaren spoke of the preacher as an evangelist and a teacher on several occasions, his most common image of a preacher was that of a prophet or herald. In an address to the Baptist Union in 1875 he said,

> If we had to offer to the world a gospel of rites, the form of our ministry would be sacerdotal. If we had to offer a gospel of thoughts, it would be professorial and didactic. But we have a gospel of fact, and therefore we preach. Not we perform, not we argue—we preach. The metaphor in the words is full of instruction. We are heralds, criers, tellers of a message. We have not evolved it from our own brains, we have received it from the King.[114]

Sometimes, he did not use the word "herald," but rather he pictured the preacher as a servant speaking God's message to the people. As an example, he stated in one address,

> There must be in it the *tone of one who is faithfully delivering a message*, rather than of one who is speaking his own thoughts. One secret of power lies here, that the whole manner, bearing, and utterance of a man shall seem to say, "I received of the Lord that which I delivered unto you." When listeners gain the impression that we are reporting realities which we have seen and handled, they will listen.[115]

As a herald, the preacher should proclaim practical applications from a text, bring the truths of Scripture to bear on the world, and boldly speak Scripture despite major opinions.[116] Because the preacher is a herald, Maclaren believed that God speaks through the preacher to the congregation.[117] He was known to pray in the service, "May this not be a mere meeting of men to listen to a man, but the gathering of God's children to listen to His voice."[118] The heralding aspect of preachers make them similar, but not identical, to the Old Testament prophets.

As an evangelist, the preacher conveys Christ, the only one who can save. As a teacher, the preacher communicates Scripture, the only message

---

114. Maclaren, "Gospel for the Day," 13.
115. Maclaren, "Gospel for the Day," 14. Emphasis original.
116. Maclaren, "Old Preacher on Preaching," 36–37.
117. Maclaren, "Old Preacher on Preaching," 37.
118. McLaren, *Dr. McLaren of Manchester*, 69.

Life Lessons and Preaching Practices

that can transform. Then, as a herald, the preacher stands as God's messenger and speaks as if God is speaking through him to the audience. Maclaren had a high view of preaching that included a concept of the preacher as an evangelist, teacher, and herald.

Outside of his lecture "An Old Preacher on Preaching," Maclaren added additional insights into his preaching method and what he believed contributed to his success. First, he preached extemporaneously. Maclaren wanted to connect to his audience, and he thought the connection waned when preachers rely too heavily on pulpit notes. In fact, in one lecture to young pastors, he became so passionate about the importance of extemporaneous preaching that he hyperbolically yelled out, "Burn your manuscripts!"[119] He believed he could not preach at all if he could not look people in the eyes. Therefore, Maclaren did not bring any notes into the pulpit nor did he write out a full manuscript beforehand. While this worked well for him, he acknowledged that such an extreme method would not be effective for every preacher. Nevertheless, one cannot read Maclaren without concluding that his willingness to preach unscripted from the pulpit, rather than being bound to a manuscript, improved his ability to move audiences.

Second, he kept Christ at the heart—the heart of the preacher and the sermon. More than anything else, Maclaren emphasized a relationship with Jesus as the source of preaching power. He believed that before the pastor stands up on Sunday, he must kneel alone with Jesus during the week. Maclaren said,

> It must be straight from Jesus Christ that we must get our power. There, within the veil, where He is, we must dwell, if any radiance is to be on our faces when we come among men. In many a hidden hour of quiet communion, in many a toilsome hour of patient thought, we must learn to know Him at first hand, as He only discloses Himself to the solitary soul waiting before Him. A life hidden with Christ in God is the indispensable condition of a life revealing Christ in the world. . . . All our power, of whatever kind it be, is His gift; let us keep close besides Him and we shall not lack.[120]

After a preacher spends personal time with Jesus daily, he must uphold Jesus in every sermon no matter where his biblical text is found.

---

119. McLaren, *Dr. McLaren of Manchester*, 74.
120. Maclaren, "Inaugural Address," 21.

The final major characteristic of Maclaren's preaching is his ability to make text-grounded applications from both the New and Old Testament. Maclaren himself stated of the preacher,

> He has to direct the searchlight on individual sins, especially those prevalent in the class from whom his hearer are [sic] drawn. He has to apply the measure of the sanctuary to worldly maxims which his hearers take for axioms, and to practices which they think legitimate because they are popular. . . . The true church must always be remonstrant, protestant, a standing rebuke to the world, till the world has accepted and applied the principles of the Gospel to personal and social life. And the preacher who does not give voice to the church's protest fails in one of his plainest and chiefest duties.[121]

Maclaren was a man with a passion for teaching the Bible and for connecting its truths to his audience. He believed the Bible still speaks relevant wisdom to contemporary problems because the reality of sin remains in people's hearts. Similarly, since the gospel is the only solution to sin, the gospel ought to be spoken no matter how sin manifests itself. He was clear that success in application does not succeed by rhetoric but by the power of the gospel. To one group of pastors he said,

> You may shiver to pieces all intellectual defences [sic], but the garrison still gathers unsubdued into the central citadel of the heart. You cannot take it by batteries of arguments. Another power alone will make the flag flutter down. Faith is an act of the will as well as of the understanding. Therefore, not logic, but the exhibition of Christ in His love and power evokes it. Ah! [sic] brethren, we are often so busy in proving the gospel that we forget to preach it; so anxious to get at men's hearts through their understandings, that all our time and strength are spent in hewing the passage and none left to impel the Gospel through it.[122]

He argued that if a person's preaching is not powerfully applied, it is because the preacher did not rely on Christ's power.[123]

Maclaren had a high view of preaching that centered on the careful exposition of Scripture and was characterized by personal devotion to Christ and the gospel, diligent work in the study, powerful delivery, and

---

121. Maclaren, "Old Preacher on Preaching," 36.
122. Maclaren, "Gospel for the Day," 23.
123. Maclaren, *Secret of Power*, 9–14.

text-grounded applications that find their ultimate end in Christ. After reviewing Maclaren's life and preaching, his methodology of preaching and applying the major literary genres in the Bible can now be studied.

DISCUSSION QUESTIONS

1. What impact did Maclaren's mother, father, and wife have on his preaching and pastoral ministry? What impact do the people around you have on you as a person and preacher?
2. What key habits did Maclaren learn that improved his preaching ability? How can you cultivate these habits in your own practice?
3. Maclaren spoke of preachers as being evangelist, teachers, and heralds. Do you agree? Why or why not?

2

Pictures and Models
Narratives

"The remarkable thing in the story is the picture it gives us of Christ."
—Alexander Maclaren

What is your favorite story from the Bible? Even if you did not grow up in church, you might still know the names or general plots of one or more stories from Scripture. Narratives account for thirty to forty percent of the Old Testament, as well as a substantial part of the New Testament. With a majority of God's Word being the genre of narrative, preachers and teachers must learn how to handle narrative texts or their ministry will be void of a major section of biblical revelation.

However, numerous challenges make applying the stories of the Bible difficult. First, you have the obstacle of historical distance. There are people, places, and customs in Bible stories that are so old that we simply do not relate to them easily. Second, there is the obstacle of geographic distance. Listeners today frequently are unfamiliar with the geography and political landscape of the Bible. Furthermore, Scripture describes historical figures who do not have a European or Western mindset. Third, there is the obstacle of literary distance. The Bible was written by authors who not only wrote in Hebrew and Greek but also used literary customs that are different from what we are accustomed to when we read stories today.[1]

Even when a preacher understands the content of a biblical passage, he still might present a narrative in a way that sacrifices its narrative spirit on the altar of a more conventional sermon structure. Sermons on biblical stories often sound more like a doctor dissecting a dead text than a preacher proclaiming a story about the living God. Kaiser put it well:

> Nothing can be more discouraging and disheartening for contemporary believers gathered to hear the Word of God than to listen to a simple recounting or bare description of an Old Testament or Gospel narrative. . . . There is the extreme of that dry, detached, and boring recital which makes the greatest ado about the most insignificant nothingness.[2]

For these reasons, Majors argues, "Narrative is the most common genre in the Bible, and more text-inaccurate interpretation is made with it than with any other genre."[3] Not only understanding but also communicating the biblical stories in a pertinent manner is a formidable task.

These problems are compounded when preachers attempt to make text-grounded applications about narratives. Appropriate applications often are not explicitly stated by the author in a story. Instead, the author uses story elements to highlight to what the reader should pay attention. Because these elements can be geared toward ancient audiences, contemporary readers can easily misapply certain details of the text in ways which the author never intended. The result is spiritualizing, allegorizing, moralizing, and speculative character analysis.[4]

For these reasons, preachers face a daunting task when making text-grounded applications from the stories of the Bible. A model is needed for how to apply this portion of Scripture. Alexander Maclaren can serve as one such model. Maclaren did not base his applications on a surface-level evaluation of the characters or on random details in a story. He based his applications on the theological lesson that the biblical author intended for his readers to learn.

1. Osborne, *Hermeneutical Spiral*, 203–12. Cf. Kaiser Jr., *Preaching and Teaching from the Old Testament*, 64.
2. Kaiser Jr., *Toward an Exegetical Theology*, 197, 200.
3. Majors, "Text-Accurate Applications," 80.
4. Mathewson, *Old Testament Narrative*, 99; Majors, "Text-Accurate Applications," 79.

HOW TO MODEL MACLAREN IN THE NARRATIVES

Maclaren's preaching on the biblical narratives has received more critical acclaim than his sermons from any other genre. When his *Expositions of Holy Scripture* was released, one reviewer found his sermons from 2 Kgs through Esther to be "useful" because of their "simplicity, directness, and force."[5] More recent scholarship has praised his longer volume on Genesis.[6] Both Pitts and Blackwood argue that it is the best volume in his entire *Expositions of Holy Scripture*.[7] His success in application was grounded upon his view of the stories as both true depictions of historical events and theological messages. He believed the primary purpose of the Bible stories is not to give moral lessons but to unfold God's redemptive plan in history. Therefore, preachers should seek to learn from Maclaren how likewise to apply narratives.

For Maclaren, the narratives suggest a theological "thought" or a "lesson" that can be "deduced" by careful readers.[8] The biblical authors accomplish this purpose through multiple means. First, a narrative can serve as an example of a theological truth, as well as reveal the consequences of either following or ignoring that truth.[9] Second, stories tell theology in such a way that it stamps the theology upon the hearts of the reader.[10] Finally, narratives are prophetic, pointing to Jesus. Maclaren argued in one sermon, "The history of Israel is a parable and a prophecy as well as a history."[11] Indeed, he saw this as the main thrust of the entire Old Testament.[12] Thus, the focus of the stories is not the nation of Israel nor the human actors. The stories focus on God and his works.[13] Since the focus of all the Bible stories is God, the theological point of the text is the key to applying Old and New Testament narratives. When preaching from a biblical story, consider the following four steps to understanding the passage and bringing clarity to the audience.

5. Anonymous, "New Literature" (1908), 478.
6. Maclaren, *Genesis*.
7. Pitts, "Alexander Maclaren," 7; Blackwood, *Biographical Preaching for Today*, 115.
8. Maclaren, *Second Kings from Chapter VIII, and Chronicles, Ezra, and Nehemiah*, 118.
9. Maclaren, *Genesis*, 45.
10. Maclaren, *Exodus, Leviticus and Numbers*, 8.
11. Maclaren, *Exodus, Leviticus and Numbers*, 291.
12. Maclaren, *Exodus, Leviticus and Numbers*, 41–42.
13. Maclaren, *Deuteronomy, Joshua, Judges, Ruth, and First Book of Samuel*, 198.

PICTURES AND MODELS

1. Understand the Contents of the Story

Preachers can learn how to understand and explain biblical stories from reading the sermons of Maclaren. First, be careful to exegete and explain the text within its larger literary context as well as the historical context of the passage. The context includes both its placement in redemptive history and its historical-cultural background.[14] Instead of speaking in the style of an uninterested lecturer, vividly retell the story so that the audience can "feel the force" of the narrative.[15] For example, Maclaren said of Moses' encounter with Pharaoh,

> At the very moment when Pharaoh was blustering and threatening, and Moses was bearding him, giving back scorn for scorn, the latter heard with the inward ear the voice which made Pharaoh's words empty wind, and gave him the assurance and commands contained in verses 1 to 3 ... Moses' conviction, which he knew to be not his own thought but God's revelation of His purposes, pointed first to the final blow which was to finish Pharaoh's resistance. He had been vacillating between compliance and refusal, like an elastic ball which yields to compression and starts back to its swelling rotundity as soon as the pressure is taken off. But at last he will collapse altogether, like the same ball when a slit is cut into it, and it shrivels into a shapeless lump.... With the new divine command swelling in his heart, Moses speaks his last word to Pharaoh, towering above him in righteous wrath, and dwindling his empty threats into nothingness. What a contrast between the impotent rage of the despot, with his vain threat, 'Thou shalt die,' and the unblenching boldness of the man with God at his back![16]

In another sermon regarding the Israelites crossing the Jordan River, he explained the text by saying,

> The army of Israel was just beginning a hard conflict under an untried leader. Behind them the Jordan barred their retreat, in front of them Jericho forbade their advance. Most of them had never seen a fortified city, and had no experience nor engines for a siege. So we may well suppose that many doubts and fears shook the courage of

---

14. Maclaren, *Genesis*, 42–43; Maclaren, *Exodus, Leviticus and Numbers*, 37; Maclaren, *Sermons Preached in Manchester: Third Series*, 95.

15. Maclaren, *Second Samuel and the Books of Kings to Second Kings VII*, 334. One reviewer wrote that Maclaren had the "power to make the past live again." Faunce, "Expository Preaching. III," 322.

16. Maclaren, *Exodus, Leviticus and Numbers*, 34–35.

the host, as it drew around the doomed city. Their chief had his own heavy burden. He seems to have gone apart to meditate on what his next step was to be. Absorbed in thought, he lifts up his eyes mechanically, as brooding men will, not expecting to see anything, and is startled by the silent figure of 'a man with a sword drawn' in his hand, close beside him. There is nothing supernatural in his appearance; and the immediate thought of the leader is, 'Is this one of the enemy that has stolen upon my solitude?' So, promptly and boldly, he strides up to him with the quick challenge: 'Whose side are you on? Are you one of us, or from the enemy's camp?' And then the silent lips open. 'Upon neither the one nor the other. I am not on your side, you are on mine, for as Captain of the Lord's host, am I come up.' And then Joshua falls on his face, recognises [sic] his Commander-in-Chief, owns himself a subordinate, and asks for orders. 'What saith my Lord unto his servant?'[17]

When providing the context of the story, use vivid language as well. The context essentially can become a story in itself.[18] This imaginative retelling of the story is a method that was quite rare before Maclaren began to preach. His style was imitated by younger preachers because they saw how it contributed to his preaching power.[19] It likewise freshens the ears of congregations today.

2. Find the Author's Theological Lesson

After retelling the story in a manner that the audience can understand and experience, "draw lessons" for them. These lessons should not be random insights you had while reading the passage. Rather, focus on what the biblical author intended for his hearers to learn from that portion of Scripture.[20] Maclaren usually marked this shift from story explanation to theological discussion by changing his pronouns. He spoke in more universal terms rather than referring to the people and events in the text. Similarly, the first-person plural pronoun ought to be used throughout when you are describing the theological lessons of the text. These stylistic changes distinguish

---

17. Maclaren, *Deuteronomy, Joshua, Judges, Ruth, and First Book of Samuel*, 123–24.
18. Maclaren, *Exodus, Leviticus and Numbers*, 34; Maclaren, *Conquering Christ*, 163–64; Maclaren, *Esther, Job, Proverbs and Ecclesiastes*, 7.
19. Williamson, *Life of Alexander Maclaren*, 202–3. Cf. Pace, "Alexander Maclaren," 78.
20. Maclaren, *Second Samuel and the Books of Kings to Second Kings VII*, 149.

for the audience that you have moved from explanation of the story to theological discussion.

The characters themselves should not be the focal point of the sermons. Focus on the theological lesson the author is teaching about God and his relationship with humanity. The author's theological proposition is essential to proper application from the narratives because, while the narrative is couched in historical and cultural garb, the theology is eternal and true for all audiences. This was the focus of Maclaren's preaching. In one sermon he said, "Now dear friends! [sic] the letter of the example may be put aside; the spirit of it must be observed."[21] He did not force a theological proposition into a narrative. Instead, he carefully exegeted the text first, found the universal truth the author purposed for his readers to learn, and presented the fruit of his exegesis to his hearers.

Maclaren generally treated each story as if it taught one main theological proposition. The scenes and plot progression helped explain, enforce, or apply the theological point of the whole narrative.[22] He usually stated multiple theological lessons, but these were not unconnected ideas; they all helped enforce the major point of the text.

The plot of a narrative can suggest a theological thought in multiple different ways.[23] Sometimes the plot depicts God's character and human sinfulness, which do not change no matter the era or location.[24] At other times, the characters themselves are the vehicles by which the author conveys his theological proposition. Specifically, dialogue can reveal a lesson the reader is supposed to learn.[25] Descriptions of what the characters did or descriptions of what the characters were like can give important theological clues as well.[26]

However, use caution when trying to connect the actions of characters directly to audiences today. Maclaren had a strong sense of *progressive*

---

21. Maclaren, *Second Kings from Chapter VIII, and Chronicles, Ezra, and Nehemiah*, 342.

22. E.g. Maclaren, *Second Kings from Chapter VIII, and Chronicles, Ezra, and Nehemiah*, 326–34.

23. Maclaren, *Exodus, Leviticus and Numbers*, 370 and 372; Maclaren, *Deuteronomy, Joshua, Judges, Ruth, and First Book of Samuel*, 229 and 331; Maclaren, *Second Samuel and the Books of Kings to Second Kings VII*, 19–20.

24. Maclaren, *Genesis*, 53–55; Maclaren, *Deuteronomy, Joshua, Judges, Ruth, and First Book of Samuel*, 231–32.

25. E.g. Maclaren, *Deuteronomy, Joshua, Judges, Ruth, and First Book of Samuel*, 262.

26. Alexander Maclaren, *Unchanging Christ*, 131; Maclaren, *Genesis*, 49.

revelation, the idea that God inspired multiple authors to write Scripture over the course of several centuries. He understood that the Old Testament authors were writing to a people under the old covenant and were connected to old covenant stipulations.[27] Similarly, parts of the Gospels and Acts describe historical events unique to their time in history. Nevertheless, this does not mean such stories are not applicable now. Tracing the progressive revelation of a theme can show how the theological lesson of a text is still true today.[28] For example, Old Testament saints were saved by faith in God similar to modern believers.[29] Old Testament events, such as the exodus experience, can even convey theological truths that are found in the New Testament.[30]

One way Maclaren transitioned Old Testament applications for New Testament believers was to take a physical blessing or curse in an Old Testament narrative and apply it spiritually to Christians. He once told his audience that

> the children of Israel in the wilderness, surrounded by miracle, had nothing which we do not possess. They had some things in an inferior form; their sustenance came by manna, ours comes by God's blessing on our daily work, which is better. Their guidance came by this supernatural pillar; ours comes by the reality of which that pillar was nothing but a picture. And so, instead of fancying that men thus led were in advance of us, we should learn that these, the supernatural manifestations, visible and palpable, of God's presence and guidance were the beggarly elements: 'God having provided some better thing for us that they without us should not be made perfect.' With this explanation of the relation between the miracle and symbol of the Old, and the reality and standing miracle of the New Covenants, let us look at the eternal truths, which are set before us in a transitory form, in this cloud by day and fiery pillar by night.[31]

Like Maclaren, be slow to equate Israel's promises, commands, and even circumstances to New Covenant believers. Instead, convey how the theological purpose of the text is true and still touches lives today. The theological

---

27. Maclaren, *Second Kings from Chapter VIII, and Chronicles, Ezra, and Nehemiah*, 287.

28. Maclaren, *Genesis*, 31.

29. Maclaren, *Conquering Christ*, 165–66.

30. Maclaren, *Exodus, Leviticus and Numbers*, 291–92.

31. Maclaren, *Exodus, Leviticus and Numbers*, 305–6.

Pictures and Models

proposition serves as a suitable bridge because it remains true for all people throughout time and circumstances.

3. Look for How the Story Points to Jesus.

Because the purpose of many narratives is to show humanity's sinfulness or to encourage a right relationship with God, Maclaren frequently preached about how Christ is God's ultimate answer, motivation, or pattern for Christians to follow. This is a pattern preachers today ought to emulate. In fact, the person and work of Christ is the main point of not merely the entire New Testament but also of the entire Old Testament as well. Maclaren said,

> All other questions about the Old Testament, however interesting and hotly contested, are of secondary importance compared with this. Is its chief purpose to prophesy of Christ, His atoning death, His kingdom and church, or is it not? The New Testament has no doubt of the answer.[32]

If the preacher finds the natural connection to Christ, then to preach about Christ from the narratives does "not in the slightest degree vary the essential force and meaning" of the text.[33]

However, a word of caution is in order. Be careful not to harm the text by forcing Christ into every detail of a story. Instead ask, "How does the author point to Christ?" Maclaren models multiple methods of making appropriate connections to Jesus. Like Maclaren, you can point to how an Old Testament text is used in the New Testament.[34] Christ can also be the ultimate example of what it looks like to follow the lesson of a story.[35] In the Gospels, Jesus occasionally quoted a biblical story or taught lessons similar to other biblical authors.[36] Christ, in effect, gives preachers his own way of making connections to him. In the Old Testament, how God acted on behalf of Israel may give clues as to how Christ acts on behalf of the church.[37] In a few sermons, Maclaren simply stated that what was true for Israel in the Old Testament is still true for Christians now. For example,

---

32. Maclaren, *Exodus, Leviticus and Numbers*, 42.
33. Maclaren, *Sermons Preached in Manchester: Third Series*, 106.
34. Maclaren, *Conquering Christ*, 142.
35. Maclaren, *Sermons Preached in Manchester: Third Series*, 108.
36. Maclaren, *Exodus, Leviticus and Numbers*, 24–25.
37. Maclaren, *Secret of Power*, 262–63.

following God in the Old Testament is equivalent to following Christ in the New Testament.[38] However, Maclaren's most frequent method of preaching Christ from narratives was typology.[39] Christological typology occurs when a person, object, or practice in the Old Testament stands as a pre-incarnate example of who Christ is or what he does. While typology can be difficult to handle appropriately, when a person, object, or practice in a narrative is obviously related to Christ through typology, do not miss the opportunity to point that out to your audience.

4. Apply the Theological Lesson of the Narrative.

Only after retelling the story, giving its theological proposition, and pointing to Christ are you ready to apply the text to your audience. *Application* was defined by Maclaren as impressing the truth upon your hearers.[40] Maclaren was lauded for how he tied his applications to the explanation of his narrative text. He allowed the vivid retelling of the story to affect his hearers in the same way it would have affected the original audiences. Then, his main applications came only after the text had been fully explained. Williamson argued that this was a new method of preaching narratives that Maclaren pioneered, and he was imitated by many afterward.[41] Pace likewise states,

> A notable strength of Maclaren's method in preaching narrative texts was the way he maintained the original format of the text by telling the story. Maclaren allowed the power of the narrative drama to impact his listeners in the way it would have affected the original recipients of the text. Maclaren then proceeded to identify "general lessons" that could be derived from the salient points of the narrative.[42]

Blackwood similarly insists that Maclaren's preaching is the "ideal method" for preaching a sermon about a biblical character.[43]

---

38. Maclaren, *Secret of Power*, 258; Maclaren, *Exodus, Leviticus and Numbers*, 11.
39. Maclaren, *Exodus, Leviticus and Numbers*, 11, 42, 44, 307, and 352.
40. Maclaren, *Second Kings from Chapter VIII, and Chronicles, Ezra, and Nehemiah*, 337.
41. Williamson, *Life of Alexander Maclaren*, 202–3.
42. Pace, "Alexander Maclaren," 78.
43. Blackwood, *Biographical Preaching*, 115.

Pictures and Models

Maclaren made several comments in his sermons that indicate his commitment to grounding his applications on the author's theological proposition of the text. He denounced applications that are not within the bounds of the text's theological thrust.[44] He also appealed to the theological proposition as justification for applying a text outside the bounds of the original setting but within the bounds of its theological message.[45] Even when a text has several minor applications, he focused on the central application that stemmed from the central theological proposition of the narrative.[46] Furthermore, he treated the details in the narrative as applicable only if they were connected to the main theological lesson the author meant to convey.[47] Only on rare occasions did he say he was "dismissing" the literary context and apply the theological lesson directly to the people in his day.[48] For Maclaren, the theological proposition was essential for proper application.

It may be appropriate to change your style of speaking when applying the text in order to indicate to your audience that you are applying the text to their lives. This was Maclaren's practice when preaching. Express applications as a direct command or personal obligation, such as saying people "should," "ought," "must," or "shall" do something. Use a speaker tag such as "Oh!" or "Brothers" to grab their attention. Include second-person pronouns. Rhetorical questions are also a useful means to incite the congregation to action. Maclaren's most frequent mode of expressing application from narrative texts came in the form of conditional sentences. For example, on 2 Chron 29:18–31 he said, "If we are chosen to be His ministers, we have solemn responsibilities. If we are to burn incense before Him, our censers need to be bright and free from strange fire. If we are the lights of the world, our business is to shine."[49] In these ways, he signaled to his hearers that what the text taught applied directly to their lives.

Maclaren had multiple means of finding application for his sermon which preachers today can emulate. If the theological lesson of the text is found throughout Scripture, apply the principle directly to the lives of

---

44. Maclaren, *Deuteronomy, Joshua, Judges, Ruth, and First Book of Samuel*, 114.
45. Maclaren, *Conquering Christ*, 142–43.
46. Maclaren, *Deuteronomy, Joshua, Judges, Ruth, and First Book of Samuel*, 19.
47. Maclaren, *Deuteronomy, Joshua, Judges, Ruth, and First Book of Samuel*, 28.
48. Maclaren, *Sermons Preached in Manchester: Third Series*, 96.
49. Maclaren, *Second Kings from Chapter VIII, and Chronicles, Ezra, and Nehemiah*, 232.

the hearers.⁵⁰ Otherwise, show how the theological proposition develops through the course of progressive revelation. Search the New Testament epistles to see if the New Testament authors either directly quoted the story or said something similar to the theological main point of the story. If so, look to these passages as guides for applications.⁵¹

Since God and human sinfulness do not change despite transitions in historical eras or cultures, base your applications on the experiences your audience have in common with the original audiences. One way to do this is by connecting your hearers to one or more characters in the story. Show how biblical characters share similar experiences and emotions with people today. For example, Maclaren said in one sermon,

> Then we are sure that they had sorrow and joy, strife and love, toil and rest, like the rest of us, that whether their days were longer or shorter they were filled much as ours are, that whatever was the pattern into which the quiet threads of their life was woven it was, warp and weft, the same yarn as ours. In broad features every human life is much the same. Widely different as the clothing of these grey fathers in their tents, with their simple contrivances and brief records, is from that of cultivated busy Englishmen to-day, the same human form is beneath both.⁵²

And in another sermon he contended,

> The period of oppression was to stir them up out of their comfortable nest, and make them willing to risk the bold dash for freedom. Is not that the explanation, too, of the similar times in our lives? It needs that we should experience life's sorrows and burdens, and find how hard the world's service is, and how quickly our Goshens may become places of grievous toil, in order that the weak hearts, which cling so tightly to earth, may be detached from it, and taught to reach upwards to God.⁵³

The physical experiences of characters do not have to be completely mirrored in modern listeners. Sometimes, a physical action, consequence, or experience can be equated to a person's spiritual life.⁵⁴ For example, the

---

50. Maclaren, *Conquering Christ*, 139; Maclaren, *Genesis*, 51.

51. Maclaren, *Conquering Christ*, 141; Maclaren, *Genesis*, 40; Maclaren, *Deuteronomy, Joshua, Judges, Ruth, and First Book of Samuel*, 126 and 230.

52. Maclaren, *Genesis*, 47.

53. Maclaren, *Exodus, Leviticus and Numbers*, 4.

54. Maclaren, *Exodus, Leviticus and Numbers*, 44.

physical actions of a character might be representative of something Christians should do or not do spiritually.[55] Thus, Maclaren found appropriate applications by finding how the theological proposition speaks to common human experiences witnessed by both the original audience and the hearers of his day.

Maclaren had several common experiences that he routinely pulled upon in order to make appropriate applications from narratives. Modern Christians share the same faith in God, presence of God, and obligations to follow God as the original audience did. Maclaren said,

> Their faith, which grasped the God revealed in their creed, was the same as our faith, though the creed which their faith grasped was only an outline sketch of yours and mine. But at all times and in all generations, the element and essence of the religious life has been the same—that is, the realizing sense of the living divine presence, the effort and aspiration after communion with Him, and the quiet obedience and conformity of the practical life to His will. And so we can reach out our hands across all the centuries to this pre-Noachian, antediluvian patriarch, dim amongst the mists, and feel that he too is our brother.[56]

Since God remains the same, the faithful actions of the saints in both Old and New Testaments can serve as examples of how to apply the theological truth practically. While the main topic of the sermons should rarely be a simple exhortation to be like a character, once the theological proposition is found, the characters can illustrate practical applications of the theological proposition. By looking at how characters in the stories related to God, Maclaren was able to make applications that demonstrated how his audience could relate to God as well.

The universal nature of God was not the only bridge Maclaren used to make applications from the narratives. Sinful attitudes and actions in the narratives continue to be experienced in contemporary society. Because of this fact, what the narrative teaches about sin can be applied to audiences in any era or culture. Maclaren argued in one sermon, "The history of Israel is a picture on the large scale of what befalls every man."[57] The sinful acts of some characters are prototypical of how all humans respond to

---

55. Maclaren, *Conquering Christ*, 170; Maclaren, *Genesis*, 44.
56. Maclaren, *Genesis*, 42.
57. Maclaren, *Deuteronomy, Joshua, Judges, Ruth, and First Book of Samuel*, 22.

temptation.[58] Maclaren even believed it was a sin to fail to follow the positive example found in the text.[59] These applications are important not just to the individuals but also for society. Sinfulness is the ultimate problem in society. Society's problems are resolved by correcting the sins in individuals.[60]

Since sin is a major theme in Maclaren's applications from the narratives, Christ often appears as the ultimate application. This practice can be imitated by preachers today. Christ is the only solution to the problem of sin. Therefore, exhort hearers to not only accept Christ but also to obey the text by looking to Christ as their motivation and source of power.[61] Maclaren argued in one sermon about Christ,

> His life is our pattern. Our marching orders are brief and simple and simple: Follow your leader, and plant your feet in His footprints. That is the sum of all ethics, and the *vade mecum* for practical life. However diverse our duties and circumstances are, the principles which come out in the Divine record of that fair life and wondrous death will fit with equal closeness to us all; and so Divine and all comprehensive is it that it abides as the sufficient pattern for every class, for every stage, for every variety of character, for every era, and ever land, till the end, and beyond the end.[62]

Do not jump to moralizing or allegorizing the text, but find the theological proposition which the author purposed for his readers to learn. Then apply the text in a manner that correlates with the author's theological point. In doing so, Maclaren kept his applications in line with authorial intent. Preachers of all ages can do the same by modeling him.

MAIN TAKE-AWAYS FROM MACLAREN FOR NARRATIVES

Preachers can glean much from Maclaren on how to apply narratives in a manner that does justice to authorial intent. The primary function of the biblical stories is to teach about God, so applying a narrative based on the theological proposition of the text is the best way for the preacher to conform their applications to authorial intent. In other words, applications can

---

58. Maclaren, *Exodus, Leviticus and Numbers*, 16, 368–69.
59. Maclaren, *Conquering Christ*, 169.
60. Maclaren, *Genesis*, 52.
61. Maclaren, *Sermons Preached in Manchester: Third Series*, 106–8; Maclaren, *Second Kings from Chapter VIII, and Chronicles, Ezra, and Nehemiah*, 85, 94 and 340–41.
62. Maclaren, *Secret of Power*, 236.

fail if the preacher jumps straight to contemporary significance without considering the theological significance the author intended for the original audience. Specifically, Maclaren's applications have three qualities that are helpful for preachers seeking to make text-driven applications.

1. Connect Today's Hearers to the Original Hearers.

First, Maclaren bridged the theological proposition to the application by looking at what modern hearers have in common with the original hearers. The human experience is largely unchanged throughout history; thus, the theological lesson of a story is still relevant to today's audience in situations analogous to the original audience. The universal nature of God, humanity's relationship with God, and human sinfulness are particularly effective bridges to application. Narratives show how God acted in the past, so they also can show how God might act in similar situations in modern times. Emphasizing the commonality between the modern and ancient readers can help the audience identify with the characters of the story and see how the story applies to their lives. Maclaren does this well in his applications from narratives.

2. Use Characters as Clues for Applications.

Second, Maclaren demonstrated how to use the characters appropriately in applications from biblical stories. Characters can reveal how we should act if the theological thrust of the story is true, or they might show what an unfaithful response might be to such a lesson. The actions of characters can be helpful clues for application; however, the theological proposition remains the grounds that supports these applications.

Preachers and teachers face several problems when looking to biblical characters as clues to application. An undue focus on characters can lead audiences to feel as if the whole point of a story is to emulate a Bible character when sermons should be more focused on God's works and emulating Christ.[63] Smith put it well:

> Jesus referred to many stories in the Old Testament, and the writer of Hebrews used multiple examples in Hebrews 11. So there is value, and biblical warrant, in using Old Testament characters as

---

63. Majors, "Text-Accurate Applications," 81

examples. However, if our preaching of Old Testament narratives only advances the moral lesson of a story, then it stops short of bringing the listener to Christ and can simply become a lesson in how to be better.[64]

Fee and Stuart similarly and correctly warn, "Your task is to learn God's Word from the narratives about them, not to try to do everything that was done in the Bible. Just because someone did something, that does not mean that you have either permission or obligation to do it, too."[65] Maclaren avoided this danger by emphasizing the theological proposition of the author. Only after emphasizing the theological point of a story did he look to the characters for clues on how the theological proposition can be lived out. Preachers would do well to pay attention to his process.

3. Take the Time to Tell the Story Well.

Finally, Maclaren revealed how a vivid retelling of the story can facilitate the application of the text. Arthurs similarly points out that "vivid language appeals to the sense and re-creates experience so that we learn vicariously."[66] Sometimes, simply explaining the details of the text in a way that engages their imaginations can help people understand how the verses apply to them because it enables the audience to identify with the characters or original readers. In fact, "identification" is one of the primary rhetorical functions unique to the genre of narrative.[67] Once identification occurs between the audience and the text, applications seem more natural and obvious to them.[68] Maclaren was a master of doing just that in the biblical narratives. He explained the text in a way that made the audience feel as if they were in the scene with the characters. This captured the imagination of the audience and allowed them to see where the theological lesson of the text applied in their own lives and communities.

Maclaren's sermons can serve as a model for how to apply the stories of the Bible because he grounded his applications on authorial intent. He first exegeted the story in order to find the theological proposition the biblical author purposed for his readers to learn. Only afterward did he

---

64. Smith, *Recapturing the Voice of God*, 49.
65. Fee and Stuart, *How to Read the Bible for All Its Worth*, 93.
66. Arthurs, *Preaching with Variety*, 96.
67. Long, *Preaching and the Literary Forms of the Bible*, 74–76.
68. Osborne, *Hermeneutical Spiral*, 221.

Pictures and Models

use the unchanging nature of God and humanity, a proper understanding of the characters, and a vivid retelling of the story to apply that lesson to his audience. Biblically sound preachers and teachers ought to learn from Maclaren in this regard when writing their own expositions from the narratives of Scripture.

SERMON BREAKDOWN: "THE WATERS SAW THEE; THEY WERE AFRAID"

Maclaren's sermon "The Waters Saw Thee; They were Afraid" from Josh 3:5–17 provides a good example of his preaching from a narrative.[69] He followed the moves of the plot, end-loaded his main application, and clearly connected his text to Christ.

His sermon began immediately with a discussion of the text's context. As is typical for many of Maclaren's sermons, he did not start with a long introduction but simply began explaining his text. After giving the story's outline, he noted that some of the literary features of the story might seem unusual to his Western audience but are a "common manner of Old Testament history."[70] He argued these literary devices are not proof of scriptural error.

Maclaren then moved to his first section by stating, "Verses 5 and 6 of the chapter belong to the section which deals with the preparation."[71] He explained the verses by vividly retelling the story. At one point he said,

> There was the rushing stream, swollen as it always is in the harvest. How were they to get over? And if the people of Jericho, right over against them, chose to fall upon them as they struggled across, what could hinder utter defeat? No doubt, all that was canvassed in all sorts of tones; but no inkling of the miracle seems to have been given.[72]

From here, Maclaren switched back and forth from explaining the text to giving minor theological gems, which the author reveals in the text. When explaining the text, he referenced the Israelite people; however, when giving his theological discussions, he spoke more universally. He noted, for

---

69. Maclaren, *Deuteronomy, Joshua, Judges, Ruth, and First Book of Samuel*, 107–15.
70. Maclaren, *Deuteronomy, Joshua, Judges, Ruth, and First Book of Samuel*, 108.
71. Maclaren, *Deuteronomy, Joshua, Judges, Ruth, and First Book of Samuel*, 108.
72. Maclaren, *Deuteronomy, Joshua, Judges, Ruth, and First Book of Samuel*, 108–9.

example, that the priests were commanded to enter the river even before the miracle took place. He said, "The question is not answered till the ark is on their shoulders. To-day often sees to-morrow's duty without seeing how it is to be done."[73] Maclaren did not include any explicit application on these verses.

He then informed his audience that verses seven through seventeen are the second main section of the story but they may be divided into three parts in themselves. The first homiletical subsection began with the statement "The report of God's commands given in verses 7 and 8 is condensed, as is evident from the fuller statement of them in Joshua's address to the people, which immediately follows."[74] Maclaren emphasized the theological truth of these verses by universalizing the event for all generations and preaching in a heightened style: "What a thought to fill a man's heart with humble devotion, that God would work such a wonder in order to demonstrate that He was with him! And what a glimpse of more to follow lay in that promise, 'This day will I *begin* to magnify thee!'"[75]

Maclaren moved to verses nine through thirteen by announcing, "We may pass on, then, to the second division of the narrative; namely, Joshua's communication of God's commands to the people."[76] By "second division" he meant the second subdivision of the text's second main division. After explaining the Scripture in its context, he universalized the text by saying it is true of every "true servant of God." He began speaking in the first-person plural as well.[77] He retold the story so that the audience could imagine the scene and stopped on several occasions to highlight important literary features the author used to emphasize his purpose. He stated, "Mark, too, the long-drawn-out designation of the ark, with its accumulation of the nouns, which grammatical purists have found difficult."[78] This main section was almost exclusively an explanation and retelling of the event. While he made no explicit application here, he spoke several conditional sentences from which an application could be implied.

---

73. Maclaren, *Deuteronomy, Joshua, Judges, Ruth, and First Book of Samuel*, 109.
74. Maclaren, *Deuteronomy, Joshua, Judges, Ruth, and First Book of Samuel*, 110.
75. Maclaren, *Deuteronomy, Joshua, Judges, Ruth, and First Book of Samuel*, 110. Emphasis original.
76. Maclaren, *Deuteronomy, Joshua, Judges, Ruth, and First Book of Samuel*, 111.
77. Maclaren, *Deuteronomy, Joshua, Judges, Ruth, and First Book of Samuel*, 111.
78. Maclaren, *Deuteronomy, Joshua, Judges, Ruth, and First Book of Samuel*, 112.

Pictures and Models

Maclaren summarized verses nine through thirteen in a few sentences, explaining their purpose to emphasize the miracle to come, before moving to the final portion of the text. While this section was brief compared to the others, it was marked by a heightened passion and vivid language. Maclaren changed his preaching style here because the Hebrew in these verses indicated a heightened passion and style, and he told this fact to his audience. He described the Hebrew here as

> one long sentence, like the roll of an Atlantic wave, or long-drawn shout of triumph, masses together the stages of the march . . . the naked feet of the priests were dipped in the water. What a hush of almost painful expectation would fall on the gazers! Then, with a rush of triumph, the sentence pours on, like a river escaping from some rocky gorge, and tells the details of the transcendent fact.[79]

Maclaren captured the spirit of the story's climax by how he painted the Hebrew of this text.

Now that the text had been explained, he disclosed the theological truth the biblical author intended his readers to learn. Maclaren explicitly told his audience that this text has two propositions, and he showed them where they are found: "From verses 7 and 10 we learn the purpose of this miracle as being twofold. It was intended to stamp the seal of God's approbation on Joshua, and to hearten the people by the assurance of God's fighting for them."[80] After briefly explaining what this lesson would have meant to the original readers, he bridged the gap with his audience by emphasizing God's unchanging relationship with His people. In doing so, Maclaren argued the theological truths of the text are as applicable to his hearers as they were to the Israelites:

> God does not disdain to duplicate His wonders, even for very unworthy servants. The unchanging, long-suffering patience, and the unwearied strength to which all generations in succession can turn with confidence, are wonderfully set forth by these two miracles. And though we have passed into the higher stage, where miracles have ceased, the principle which dictated the parallelism still holds good.[81]

---

79. Maclaren, *Deuteronomy, Joshua, Judges, Ruth, and First Book of Samuel*, 113.
80. Maclaren, *Deuteronomy, Joshua, Judges, Ruth, and First Book of Samuel*, 114.
81. Maclaren, *Deuteronomy, Joshua, Judges, Ruth, and First Book of Samuel*, 114.

Maclaren now delivered his main application. The application was marked by the use of the first-person plural pronoun and a change from statements of fact to statements of possibility. His application in this sermon was shorter than in other sermons on narratives. It began immediately after he stated the theological lesson: "... and we too can look back to all these ancient wonders, and be sure that they are done over and over again according to our needs. 'As we have heard, so have we seen,' might have been Israel's song that day, as it may be ours every day."[82] Maclaren concluded by connecting the narrative to Christ. He vocalized that the story illustrates Christ's work on the cross for humanity. His last statement left that fact ringing in the ears of his audiences:

> We may well allow faith and hope to discern ... an emblem of that dark flood that rolled between the host of God and their home, and was dried up as soon as the pierced foot of the Christ touched its cold waters ... Christ has gone up before us. He has shaken His hand over the river, and caused men to go over dry shod.[83]

DISCUSSION QUESTIONS

1. Why is discovering the theological point of a narrative a vitally important step to take prior to application? What is the danger in applying a character's actions to today without first considering the author's theological purpose?

2. Where should you look in a narrative to find clues regarding the theological lesson intended by the author?

3. Try finding text-grounded applications for Judg 13, 1 Sam 4, Mark 5:1–20, and Acts 28:1–10.

---

82. Maclaren, *Deuteronomy, Joshua, Judges, Ruth, and First Book of Samuel*, 114.
83. Maclaren, *Deuteronomy, Joshua, Judges, Ruth, and First Book of Samuel*, 114–15.

3

Shadows of What Is to Come
Law

"The Lawgiver is visible behind the law."
—Alexander Maclaren

Have you ever tried to read the Bible starting in the book of Genesis? Did you finish? If not, where did you stop? If you are like most people who have tried to read the Bible starting in Genesis, and you did not finish, you most likely stopped when you hit Leviticus, Numbers, and Deuteronomy. This is not a recent struggle for Christians either. In fact, the difficulty of seeing the relevance of law passages has sparked the rise of numerous heresies and heretics. Even people who specialize in these books don't tread them easily. These works are incredibly hard to read and apply as Christians.

All the narrative obstacles from the previous chapter still hold true for law, but they are amplified. Moseley correctly describes the experience of some readers when they reach the law portions of the Old Testament:

> At that point the engine sputters and their excitement about reading through the Bible begins to lose altitude. By the time they reach Leviticus they have stopped soaring and started crawling. They read about sacrifices that are no longer offered, a priesthood that no longer exists, and laws they are not obligated to obey. All

of that and more is described in tedious detail, so some people ask, "Why is this in the Bible?"[1]

Five common myths abound regarding the Law which deter people from reading and teaching these chapters: it involves obsolete ritualistic trivia, it shows ancient interests that do not speak to the modern day, it is inferior to Christ's law of love, it contains literary forms that readers today do not understand, and it presents a picture of God that is objectionable to modern society.[2] Some also fallaciously treat the law as mere regulations and restrictions meant to gain God's favor. Therefore, they argue that this portion of Scripture is no longer applicable to Christians who have gained God's favor in Christ.[3] In summary, the law texts are filled with ceremonial and civil minutia that to many seem no longer applicable to Christians today.

Despite the difficulties in preaching from Old Testament law, the modern church needs to hear from this portion of Scripture. It is still God's revelation to his people. Furthermore, the law teaches about God's character and man's proper response to God. Preachers should not neglect the law portions of Scripture. Alexander Maclaren's sermons can help preachers visualize how to interpret and apply the law in a way that is meaningful to their audiences. In fact, Maclaren's sermons from the law texts are some of the best in his *Expositions of Holy Scripture*. He used the theological thrust of the text to accurately apply Old Testament law to his audience.

HOW TO MODEL MACLAREN IN THE LAW

Maclaren understood that preaching from law texts ought to be deeply rooted in a proper understanding of the continuity and discontinuity between the Old Covenant and the New Covenant. The law reflects the Israelite life under the Old Covenant. Many of the commands, as well as the blessings, have changed as a result of Christ's atoning work on the cross.[4] What has not changed is the theological significance which serves as the foundation for the law. Maclaren stated in one sermon, "While, then, the text primarily refers to the experience of the infant nation in the forty

---

1. Moseley, *From the Study to the Pulpit*, chapter 3, "Preaching and Teaching Old Testament Law."

2. Block, "Preaching Old Testament Law to New Testament Christians," 195.

3. Kaiser addresses this fallacy in Kaiser, *Preaching and Teaching from the Old Testament*, 139.

4. Maclaren, *Exodus, Leviticus and Numbers*, 284.

years' wanderings, it carries large truths about us all; and sets forth the true meaning and importance of life."[5]

Despite Christ's fulfillment of the law, Maclaren felt strongly that the theological lessons should still be preached because of the progressive revelation of Scripture. The psalms, prophets, and ultimately New Testament authors reflected on the law and realized that the rituals were not merely external acts but theological lessons that were universally applicable.[6] Maclaren described the law as the root that laid the necessary foundation upon which later revelation could be built.[7] The theological principles were expanded upon in greater detail by later authors, and ultimately by Christ. When this happened, the laws themselves were fulfilled. The theological lessons still stood, but the external rites are no longer required. Maclaren stated,

> In considering the Jewish sacrificial system, it is important to distinguish the symbolical from the typical value of the sacrifices. The former could scarcely be quite unnoticed by the offerers; but the latter was only gradually made plain, was probably never very generally seen, and is a great deal clearer to us, in the light of Christ, the Antitype, than it could ever have been before His coming. As symbols, the sacrifices expressed great eternal truths as to spiritual worship and communion, its hindrances, requisites, manner, and blessings. They were God's picture-book. . . . As types, they shadowed the work of Jesus Christ and its results.[8]

If the preacher views the law through the lens of progressive revelation, then he can explain the severe punishments God enacted in the Old Testament. Early in progressive revelation, the severe punishments were intended to put an exclamation point on a theological truth that was vital for future revelation.[9]

Consequently, the Old Testament stipulations were designed to be temporary placeholders until Christ came. In fact, many of the ceremonies have defects built into them that prove they were purposefully designed by God

---

5. Maclaren, *Deuteronomy, Joshua, Judges, Ruth, and First Book of Samuel*, 41.
6. Maclaren, *Exodus, Leviticus and Numbers*, 238.
7. Maclaren, *Deuteronomy, Joshua, Judges, Ruth, and First Book of Samuel*, 51, 58.
8. Maclaren, *Exodus, Leviticus and Numbers*, 233.
9. Maclaren, *Exodus, Leviticus and Numbers*. Cf. Maclaren, *Exodus, Leviticus and Numbers*, 245.

to point us to a greater reality and fulfillment in Christ.[10] Maclaren insisted, "Scaffolding is needed to erect a building, and he is not a wise man who either despises or would keep permanently standing the scaffold poles."[11] In saying the law is the scaffolding or foundation of progressive revelation, Maclaren was not implying that the law is a sub-revelation, nor was he saying that the law was less inspired than other parts of Scripture. The law is fully a revelation from God. It is also complete for what the Israelites needed in the era in which they lived. However, in the overall scope of redemptive history, the law needs the New Testament to fulfill it. He declared,

> Of course we have here an instance of the incompleteness of the Mosaic law,—or rather we may more truly say of its completeness, regard being had to the state of the world at the time. All social change hangs together. Institutions cannot be altered at a blow, without altering the stage of civilisation, of which they are the expression. 'Raw haste' is 'half-sister to delay.' What is good and necessary for one era is out of place in another.[12]

The law is as much an inspired revelation from God as other parts of Scripture, but its true significance cannot be fully realized outside of Christ. The theological lessons themselves are universal and still applicable to Christians even though Christ fulfilled many of the external requirements the law demanded. This understanding of the purpose of the law in Scripture formed the basis by which Maclaren interpreted and then applied the law to his listeners.

1. Narrate the Historical Context of the Law Passage.

Maclaren's explanations of the law were often vividly described and illustrated. In this way, he kept the law within the spirit of its narrative context. Whether it is a command or a ceremony, a teacher should view the text as a brief narrative. One should construct a story-like framework that explains the details of the text and describes it so the audience can see the event in their minds.[13] This includes explaining important Hebrew terms.[14]

---

10. Maclaren, *Exodus, Leviticus and Numbers*, 249; Maclaren, *Deuteronomy, Joshua, Judges, Ruth, and First Book of Samuel*, 51; Maclaren, *Exodus, Leviticus and Numbers*, 252.

11. Maclaren, *Exodus, Leviticus and Numbers*, 241–42.

12. Maclaren, *Exodus, Leviticus and Numbers*, 280.

13. Maclaren, *Exodus, Leviticus and Numbers*, 234–35 and 250–51.

14. Maclaren, *Deuteronomy, Joshua, Judges, Ruth, and First Book of Samuel*, 1, 40, 51,

Also, make sure to explain the larger literary context and discuss the passage in a way that stays consistent with the overall historical context.[15] The historical and cultural background of the law is vital to understanding its original meaning and purpose in Scripture, so explain how the law relates to the larger narrative of Israel's history and other cultures of its day.[16] Maclaren especially emphasized the relationship between the law and the Exodus experience.[17] The exodus event provided the grounds and the motivation to obey the law. Maclaren's application of a law text began with a careful study of the text in its literary and historical context.

2. Find the Author's Theological Purpose for the Law.

Once he explained the text, Maclaren pointed out the timeless theological point which the author intended to convey. The shift from explanation to theological reflection can be made apparent to your audience by switching from speaking about the Israelites to speaking about humanity in general. Consider your pronouns as well. Instead of using third-person plural pronouns, use first-person plural.

Maclaren very rarely applied a law text directly to Christians. A historical and theological gap exists between the Israelite audience and New Testament Christians. For that reason, the theological principle in the text provides the necessary step to move from the original audience's application of the text to how Christians should receive the law today. Maclaren once said,

> This is one of the blessings promised to obedience [in the law]. No doubt it . . . presupposes a supernatural order of things, in which material well-being was connected with moral good far more closely and certainly than we see to be the case. But the spirit and heart of the promise remain, however the form of it may have passed away.[18]

---

and 61–62; Maclaren, *Exodus, Leviticus and Numbers*, 254; Maclaren, *Leaves from the Tree of Life*, 12.

15. See Maclaren, *Exodus, Leviticus and Numbers*, 249–50 and 254–55; Maclaren, *Deuteronomy, Joshua, Judges, Ruth, and First Book of Samuel*, 2, 24–25, 47, 57–58.

16. Maclaren, *Exodus, Leviticus and Numbers*, 241, 264, and 279–80; Maclaren, *Deuteronomy, Joshua, Judges, Ruth, and First Book of Samuel*, 40–41, 51, 57.

17. Maclaren, *Exodus, Leviticus and Numbers*, 242; Maclaren, *Deuteronomy, Joshua, Judges, Ruth, and First Book of Samuel*, 22, 85.

18. Maclaren, *Exodus, Leviticus and Numbers*, 284.

Maclaren viewed the law as being symbolic of larger spiritual and theological realities. This symbolism conveys a lesson that is true today, even though the specific ritual or procedure might be fulfilled by Christ in the new covenant. These lessons often teach about God's character and how humanity can be saved from their sinfulness. Maclaren said, "The Law was the revelation of the mind, and, in some measure, of the heart, of God to man."[19] The actions, objects, images, and metaphors in the law can all be used by the author to deliver significant points. For instance, in one sermon on the various temple sacrifices, he explained,

> There were three bloody sacrifices, the sin-offering, the burnt-offering, and the peace-offering. In all three expiation was the first idea, but in the second of them the act of burning symbolised a further thought, namely, that of offering to God, while in the third, the peace-offering, there was added to both of these the still further thought of the offerer's participation with God, as symbolised by the eating of the sacrifice. So we have great verities of the most spiritual religion adumbrated in this external rite. The rind is hard and forbidding, the kernel is juicy and sweet.[20]

You can also find the theological thrust by looking at the law's purpose.[21] Sometimes the theology is "strongly insisted" by the author, while at other times it is "but a glimmer."[22] Either way, the original author intended for this theological lesson to be understood and obeyed.

Since the author wrote the law text to purposefully convey a specific theological lesson, you are not imposing a symbolic meaning onto the text but rather simply uncovering what the author wished for you to discover. By way of illustration, in speaking about the purpose of one text, Maclaren said, "Besides these purposes, it was appointed to enforce, and to make the whole fabric of the national wealth consciously rest upon, this thought contained in our text."[23] Moreover, the theological principles exist even if some of the original readers did not see them. He stated,

---

19. Maclaren, *Life of David as Reflected in His Psalms*, 8.

20. Maclaren, *Deuteronomy, Joshua, Judges, Ruth, and First Book of Samuel*, 15. Cf. Maclaren, *Exodus, Leviticus and Numbers*, 241, 256–57, 233, 252, 253.

21. Cf. His theology on the Feist of Tabernacles and the Sabbath rest. Maclaren, *Exodus, Leviticus and Numbers*, 265, 269–70.

22. Maclaren, *Deuteronomy, Joshua, Judges, Ruth, and First Book of Samuel*, 25, 27.

23. Maclaren, *Exodus, Leviticus and Numbers*, 269. Cf. Maclaren, *Deuteronomy, Joshua, Judges, Ruth, and First Book of Samuel*, 18.

> Of course, the meaning of the sacrifices was hidden from many a worshipper. They became opaque instead of transparent, and hid the great truth which they were meant to reveal. All forms labour under that disadvantage; but that they were significant in design, and largely so to devout hearts in effect, admits of no reasonable doubt. That which they signified was chiefly the putting away of sin by the sacrifice of innocent life, which stood in the place of the guilty.[24]

Not all parts of the law are designed by the author to be typological or prophetic, yet they still contain truths that Christians should understand and follow. While much of the law is not directly followed by new covenant Christians, the preacher still ought to understand and preach the theological lesson the original author intended to teach in each law text.

When preaching from the law, Maclaren not only acted as if the ceremonies and rituals as a whole teach theological truths. Maclaren actually treated each part of the ceremonies as vitally important for conveying that specific theological lesson. He did not allegorize the details of the law. Rather, a ritual as a whole carried a single theological lesson, and the details of the ritual helped convey this lesson.[25] Just as a scene contributes to the lesson of an entire narrative and a clause contributes to the lesson of an entire paragraph, so do a law's details contribute to the lesson of the entire passage.

Maclaren deployed several methods for finding the theological principle in a passage. You can follow the biblical theology of a concept found in the text to its ultimate fulfillment in the New Testament and Christ. For example, in a sermon on Lev 26:13, Maclaren once paused at the word "redeemer" and contended,

> The great central word of the New Testament has been drawn from it, viz. 'redemption,' i.e. a buying out of bondage. The Hebrew slaves in Egypt were 'delivered.' The deliverance made them a nation. God acquired them for Himself, and they became His servants. The great truths of the gospel are all there.[26]

You also can move from concrete details in the text to spiritual circumstances today. What was true of the physical sacrifices is also true for higher

---

24. Maclaren, *Exodus, Leviticus and Numbers*, 238.

25. See his discussion of the symbolism in the priestly clothing. Maclaren, *Exodus, Leviticus and Numbers*, 250. Cf. Maclaren, *Exodus, Leviticus and Numbers*, 235, 247, 254.

26. Maclaren, *Exodus, Leviticus and Numbers*, 291–92. Cf. Maclaren, *Exodus, Leviticus and Numbers*, 291–92.

spiritual realities.[27] Maclaren believed the preacher has a warrant for such a hermeneutical move because of progressive revelation.

Nevertheless, the universality of sin was the most frequent bridge Maclaren used in his theological discussions. In the same way, you can connect specific sinful circumstances in the law to similar circumstances today which deal with the same sinful problems.[28] Sin forms an appropriate theological bridge because both the original audience and audiences today struggle with the same sins. Maclaren proclaimed, "The men of that age were essentially like ourselves, and we have the same sins and spiritual necessities as they had. . . . The same consciousness is part of all of us, but how overlaid! how [sic] stifled!"[29] Furthermore, not only do humans share the same sinful longings, but they unsuccessfully deal with sin in the same ways.[30] The universality of sin is an effective bridge that pastors can use to connect the law to the church.

3. Look for How Jesus Fulfilled that Law.

Since sin is a theological bridge, preachers do not err when preaching Christ from the law. God's ultimate solution to sin is Christ's sacrifice, and the worshipful response to God once sin has been removed is a timeless response for all those who have followed God.[31] As a result, the original meaning of the law points to Christ's person and works.[32] In fact, Maclaren believed the ultimate purpose of the law was to prepare the reader for the future redemption found in Christ.[33]

Maclaren did not jump directly to Christ and preach Christ instead of the text, though. Instead, he carefully exegeted the text within its literary

---

27. Maclaren, *Exodus, Leviticus and Numbers*, 292. Cf. Maclaren, *Deuteronomy, Joshua, Judges, Ruth, and First Book of Samuel*, 76–77; Maclaren, *Exodus, Leviticus and Numbers*, 286.

28. Maclaren, *Exodus, Leviticus and Numbers*, 270 and 274; Maclaren, *Deuteronomy, Joshua, Judges, Ruth, and First Book of Samuel*, 3 and 45.

29. Maclaren, *Exodus, Leviticus and Numbers*, 257. Cf. Maclaren, *Deuteronomy, Joshua, Judges, Ruth, and First Book of Samuel*, 23–24; Maclaren, *Exodus, Leviticus and Numbers*, 266.

30. Maclaren, *Deuteronomy, Joshua, Judges, Ruth, and First Book of Samuel*, 19; Maclaren, *Exodus, Leviticus and Numbers*, 258.

31. Maclaren, *Exodus, Leviticus and Numbers*, 243.

32. Maclaren, *Deuteronomy, Joshua, Judges, Ruth, and First Book of Samuel*, 18.

33. Maclaren, *Exodus, Leviticus, and Numbers*, 41.

and historical context in order to find the theological principle of the text which Christ fulfilled. For example, on the passage regarding future Israelite prophets, Maclaren said,

> We cannot understand this passage unless we recognise that the direct reference is to the institution of the prophetic order as the standing means of imparting the reliable knowledge of God's will, possessing which, Israel had no need to turn to them 'that peep and mutter' and bring false oracles from imagined gods. But that primary reference of the words does not exclude, but rather demands, their ultimate reference to Him in whom the divine word is perfectly enshrined, and who is the bright, consummate flower of the prophetic order, which 'spake of Him,' not only in its individual predictions, but by its very existence.[34]

Christ should be preached from the law, but only through the appropriate theological thread—the one the author intended to convey by the law.

Maclaren used multiple means of connecting Christ to the law texts which expositors can emulate. Christ can be typologically seen in the people and practices in the law. He is also the promised fulfillment of the sacrifices.[35] In the sense of progressive revelation, Christ appears as the final and fullest revelation rooted in the law.[36] You can also use an analogy to compare the old covenant with the new covenant, or point to how a description of God in the law is also true in Christ.[37] Call out New Testament passages that quote your text and show its fulfillment in Christ.[38] You also can equate the Israelites' faithful obedience to the law to that of the Christian's faithful obedience to Christ.[39] Finally, use the law as an example of humanity's inability to follow God, for which Christ's forgiveness is God's gracious response.[40] All of these may be effective ways of preaching Christ, which Maclaren models well.

---

34. Maclaren, *Deuteronomy, Joshua, Judges, Ruth, and First Book of Samuel*, 18

35. For his use of typology see Maclaren, *Exodus, Leviticus and Numbers*, 233, 252–53;

36. For example, Maclaren, *Exodus, Leviticus and Numbers*, 291. Cf. Maclaren, *Deuteronomy, Joshua, Judges, Ruth, and First Book of Samuel*, 27–28, 35, and 46.

37. E.g. Maclaren, *Exodus, Leviticus and Numbers*, 244; Maclaren, *Deuteronomy, Joshua, Judges, Ruth, and First Book of Samuel*, 2.

38. Maclaren, *Exodus, Leviticus and Numbers*, 254 and 266; Maclaren, *Deuteronomy, Joshua, Judges, Ruth, and First Book of Samuel*, 32–33 and 56.

39. Maclaren, *Deuteronomy, Joshua, Judges, Ruth, and First Book of Samuel*, 76–77.

40. Maclaren, *Deuteronomy, Joshua, Judges, Ruth, and First Book of Samuel*, 12.

Maclaren did not have only one method of preaching Christ from the law. He simply sought to explain how Christ naturally is taught by a law based on a careful exegesis of the text. He found the theological principle which his text taught and used this principle as a bridge to Christ.

4. Apply the Theological Lesson of the Law.

After explaining the text and teaching its theological principle, Maclaren applied the text to his audience. Applications do not need to appear in every main point. Maclaren showed how it is appropriate in some passages to put all your applications at the end of the sermon, after the passage has been explained completely. Regardless of whether the applications are in the main point themselves or at the very end of the sermon, they ought to appear only after you exegete the text and discover the timeless theological principle.

Application sections also should be made apparent to your hearers by a change in your preaching style. While explanations and theological reflections may be general and factual, applications show more emotional and personal contact. Maclaren rarely used third-person pronouns. Second-person pronouns were used by him more consistently, especially in the form of commands.[41] He also spoke first-person plural pronouns quite frequently in his applications, pairing the pronouns with words that indicate commands or obligations such as "let," "should," "must," or "have to."[42] Speaker tags such as "brother" and "oh" also can signal the applications.[43] Maclaren argued that the preacher's purpose was not to teach passively but to take theological truths and "burn [them] into the consciousness of the people" so that the hearer "laid [them] to heart."[44] Change your style to indicate to your audience that you are no longer talking about universal theological principles from the law but rather attempting to speak directly to them.

---

41. Maclaren, *Deuteronomy, Joshua, Judges, Ruth, and First Book of Samuel*, 6, 38, 43, 49–50, 55; Maclaren, *Exodus, Leviticus and Numbers*, 277, 278–79, 289–90.

42. Maclaren, *Exodus, Leviticus and Numbers*, 272, 274, 283, 286; Maclaren, *Deuteronomy, Joshua, Judges, Ruth, and First Book of Samuel*, 6, 24, 28, 43–44.

43. Maclaren, *Deuteronomy, Joshua, Judges, Ruth, and First Book of Samuel*, 9, 42, 54, 57.

44. Maclaren, *Exodus, Leviticus and Numbers*, 243; Maclaren, *Deuteronomy, Joshua, Judges, Ruth, and First Book of Samuel*, 66.

Commands that are affirmed in the New Testament can be applied more directly. However, other commands are not directly applicable to Christians. For this reason, the theological principle is vital for applications from the law. The theological lesson of the text provides the best foundation from which to build contemporary connections. The Israelites did not mentally divide the law into civic, ceremonial, or moral distinction.[45] "Civic" refers to laws that dealt with the governance of Israel and the penalties for various crimes. "Ceremonial" laws were those that dealt with the worship of God and what makes a person unclean. Those laws that seem more universal in nature are termed "moral" laws.[46] Unfortunately, these categories sometimes are used by preachers to neglect teaching certain passages; however, even ceremonial and civic laws teach theological principles that ought to be applied regardless of which category of law the text is found. Instead of neglecting ceremonial and civil passages, apply the theological principle that serves as the foundation for these commands. In this way, Maclaren was able to preach and apply law passages that do not appear directly applicable to modern hearers.

Maclaren not only commanded his audience to obey the Lord; he also carefully explained the motivation to obey. The spirit of the law is not one of terrified submission but of loving obedience because of God's grace. The Israelites were not to obey the law in order to attain salvation. They were to obey out of love toward God after receiving salvation. Love is the motivation for modern Christians to obey God's Word as well.[47] Maclaren maintained the spirit of the law genre in his applications through stressing the relationship between love and obedience.

One unique characteristic of Maclaren's applications from the law was his willingness to apply the law to situations outside the explicit scope of the text. He believed such a homiletical move was warranted for several reasons. First, since the law is symbolic of spiritual realities, the practical application of the law could touch circumstances outside the original setting as long as it remained true to the author's theological purpose. For example, he stated in one sermon,

> There are several of the institutions and precepts of the Mosaic legislation which, though not prophetic, nor typical, have yet remarkable correspondences with lofty Christian truth. They may

---

45. Maclaren, *Exodus, Leviticus and Numbers*, 242.
46. Frame, *Doctrine of the Christian Life*, 214–15.
47. Maclaren, *Deuteronomy, Joshua, Judges, Ruth, and First Book of Samuel*, 25, 36–38.

be used as symbols, if only we remember that we are diverting them from their original purpose.[48]

In another sermon he explained,

> The words of the text simply mean that the history of the nation had sufficiently proved that God, their God, was 'above all gods.' The Canaanites and all the enemies whom Israel had fought had been beaten, and in their awe of this warrior people acknowledged that their idols had found their lord.... But the words of the text lend themselves to a wider application, and clothe in a picturesque garb the universal truth that the experience of godless men proves the futility of their objects of trust, when compared with that of him whose refuge is in God.[49]

Secondly, if the law is true of this physical world, Maclaren claimed it would be true of "higher" realities as well. He said, "May we not apply that same thought of the unbroken continuity of God's gifts to the higher region of our spiritual experience?"[50] On another occasion, he argued, "In higher matters than these our text may give us counsel as to our duty."[51] This spiritual application is part of the author's original purpose, and it is often the main application for Christians today. To give an example, he applied Lev 26:10 by saying,

> So the law for life is thankful enjoyment of the old store, and openness of mind and freedom of heart which permit its unreluctant surrender when newer harvests ripen. And the highest form of the promise of our text will be when we pass into another world, and its rich abundance is poured out into our laps. Blessed are they who can willingly put away the familiar blessings of earth, and stretch out, willingly emptied, expectant hands to meet the 'new store' of Heaven![52]

Lastly, the prophets sometimes abstracted the law to a theological principle and applied that principle to settings outside of what the law spoke.[53]

48. Maclaren, *Exodus, Leviticus and Numbers*, 281.
49. Maclaren, *Deuteronomy, Joshua, Judges, Ruth, and First Book of Samuel*, 47.
50. Maclaren, *Exodus, Leviticus and Numbers*, 286.
51. Maclaren, *Exodus, Leviticus and Numbers*, 290. Cf. Maclaren, *Deuteronomy, Joshua, Judges, Ruth, and First Book of Samuel*, 16; Maclaren, *Exodus, Leviticus and Numbers*, 291.
52. Maclaren, *Exodus, Leviticus and Numbers*, 291.
53. For example, Maclaren, *Deuteronomy, Joshua, Judges, Ruth, and First Book of Samuel*, 57–58.

Mimicking the prophets, preachers today then have the warrant to apply the theological lesson from a law text to circumstances outside the law's original scope as well.[54]

Maclaren did not apply the laws as if their only significance related to spiritual matters. He applied the law in practical ways that are faithful to the authorial intent. Applications from law texts should be direct and practical. Maclaren explicitly showed this distinction in one sermon when, after discussing the theological significance of memory, he stated, "The second and simple practical suggestion that I make is this: Remember, and let the memory lead to contrition."[55] You can model Maclaren by applying the theological principle to practices today that are analogous to those in the text.

Maclaren demonstrated two methods for making concrete applications. First, compare the circumstances that originally stimulated the law's writing to modern circumstances that are similar.[56] Look to the universality of sin and humanity's response to God to find what practices today the text can address.[57] This allows you to give concrete applications while also calling attention to God's grace in Christ. This practice also allowed Maclaren to preach on specific sins his hearers were dealing with. Second, connect the command in the law to a New Testament text that teaches a similar lesson. For instance, Maclaren applied one text which commands obedience to God by saying,

> As the words stand in our Bible, they are as follow: 'They sat down at Thy feet; every one shall receive of Thy words.' . . . It in part anticipates Christ's tender words: 'He goeth before them, and the sheep follow Him, for they know His voice.' They follow at His feet. That is the blessedness and the power of Christian morality, that it is keeping close at Christ's heels, and that instead of its being said to us, 'Go,' He says, 'Come.'. . .Yes, if you will keep close to Him, He will turn round and speak to you.[58]

---

54. Maclaren, *Exodus, Leviticus and Numbers*, 285.
55. Maclaren, *Deuteronomy, Joshua, Judges, Ruth, and First Book of Samuel*, 10.
56. E.g., Maclaren, *Deuteronomy, Joshua, Judges, Ruth, and First Book of Samuel*, 46.
57. E.g. Maclaren, *Exodus, Leviticus and Numbers*, 265–66.
58. Maclaren, *Deuteronomy, Joshua, Judges, Ruth, and First Book of Samuel*, 55–56; Cf. Maclaren, *Deuteronomy, Joshua, Judges, Ruth, and First Book of Samuel*, 49, 58; Maclaren, *Leaves from the Tree of Life*, 14–16.

Concretely apply the law to your audience by connecting the theological thrust of the passage either to similar situations of today or to New Testament passages that teach the same lesson. The spirit of the law demands practical application. However, Christ fulfilled much of the original application of the law. Maclaren's sermons show how preachers can reconcile these two demands.

MAIN TAKEAWAYS FROM MACLAREN FOR THE LAW

Maclaren's sermons mirror the structure, substance, and spirit of the law closely. Many of his sermon divisions follow natural breaks in the text, especially if it was a religious ceremony. He was careful to explain the substance of his passage, including its theological significance and context, and he usually explained how the law passage was fulfilled in Christ. Finally, he preached the spirit of the text by drilling the theological lesson into his hearer's consciousness and showing how the law applies to modern circumstances. Expository preachers can take away several lessons from Maclaren's sermons on the law.

1. Differentiate between the Old and New Covenant.

Foremost, the law was written to the Israelites under the old covenant. Be mindful, therefore, to consider the continuity and discontinuity between the original setting and new covenant believers. Even if a command seems straightforward, it is still within the context of the old covenant and connected to old covenant blessings and curses. As an example, the physical blessings promised by the law cannot be directly applied to modern circumstances. With Christ's return, these texts about physical blessings now point to greater spiritual blessings for those in Christ. The preacher is on firmer footing if he seeks to discover the theological lesson of the passage.

Maclaren did not take a law text and immediately skip to the New Testament's concept of grace. Instead, Maclaren preached the passage in its old covenant setting and then used the theological purpose of the passage as the bridge to appropriate applications. Preachers can model Maclaren's practice in this. Since the theological principle is timeless and universal, it conveys the author's purpose while also taking into account the new covenant. The substance and spirit of the law should still be maintained in the application, but it must be preserved in a manner that is consistent with the law's fulfillment in Christ.

2. Focus on Theology Not Categories.

Second, Maclaren showed that applications should be tied to the theological thrust of a passage and not to a surface-level evaluation of a text as either a civil, ceremonial, or moral duty. These categories are helpful to some extent, but they were not used by the original audience and can be overused by preachers. Maclaren's sermons provide a more helpful model. The theological proposition of the text provides the best bridge for applying the law. All portions of the law contain lessons about God and people that are timeless and thus still need to be heard by Christians today. Therefore, applications based on the theological purpose of the passage stand on firmer footing than those that are based on the civil, ceremonial, or moral implications.

3. Connect the Original Context to Applications.

Third, applications should come from a careful exegesis of the passage in its original historical and literary context. Without careful exegesis, the preacher may mistakenly apply a law to situations outside of the author's theological intent. For example, commands forbidding marriage to those outside of Israel should not be used to justify forbidding mixed-race marriages today. The theological thrust of these laws pertains to the people's religious background and not their race. The inclusion of women such as Rahab and Ruth into the people of Israel prove those prohibitions teach about religious ties in marriage. Only by tying oneself to the author's original purpose, including the author's theological purpose, can preachers apply the law in a manner that the text justifies. Maclaren's sermons demonstrated why preachers should not shy away from preaching a law text simply because it no longer seems applicable today. If the author purposed for each law to teach a timeless theological truth, then each law still has value for Christians today. Apply the law to circumstances similar to what the original audience faced.

4. Make Practical Applications in Addition to Evangelistic Appeals.

Fourth, sin and God's response to sin can be a helpful bridge from the original setting to a modern audience when preaching from the law genre. Modern humans struggle with the same sins as the ancient Israelites did, but Christ fulfilled the sacrificial system and ceremonies completely for us. Consequently, human sin and God's grace is a common theme in the law that preachers can use to apply texts to modern circumstances. Applications can show how modern hearers have both the same sin problems and the same need for God's grace in Christ as the ancient Israelites did. However, preachers should be careful not to jump immediately to Christ and therefore neglect the original application of the text. First exegete the text to understand the author's theological purpose. Only then will you see how Christ is the fulfillment of that portion of the law.

Maclaren also demonstrated how applications from the law can be concrete and not simply soteriological. Maclaren did not make his only application from the law an application of sin versus grace. Instead, he practically applied the theological thrust of the text to situations in his day that deal with similar problems and requirements. Practical applications to situations analogous to those in the text are in keeping with the spirit of Old Testament law. Maclaren showed how the law points to Christ, but he also used the law text to address the human sinfulness he saw in his day. Many of his sermons are well-balanced between explaining the text in its original context and showing how it appropriately and practically connects to believers today in Christ. As a result, preachers and teachers today would be wise to consult Maclaren's sermons whenever they find themselves in a passage from the law.

SERMON BREAKDOWN: "THE CONSECRATION OF JOY"

Maclaren's sermon "The Consecration of Joy" provides a good example of his preaching from a portion of Leviticus which typically cannot be applied directly to a New Testament believer. Leviticus 23:33–44, which describes the Festival of Booths, was his text for this particular sermon. As is usual for Maclaren's sermons, he immediately began to explain the text at hand. His introductions tended to be short, if they existed at all, as he focused more on preliminary matters regarding the text. For this sermon, he began by explaining the passage's outline and then briefly confronted several higher critical objections to the passage's unity.⁵⁹ He then spent several paragraphs explaining the details of the festival to his audience.⁶⁰ After his explanation, Maclaren moved to the theological lesson of the text. He did this by seeking the authorial intent behind the feast. He said, "What, then, was its intention? It was the commemoration of the wilderness life as the ground of rejoicing 'before the Lord.'"⁶¹ He concluded, "The feast of tabernacles was the consecration of joy."⁶² After briefly speaking about the importance of finding joy in the Lord, he stated his main theological point: "Joy is a duty to God's children."⁶³ This would be the bridge by which he would make his applications.

From this theological lesson, Maclaren drew several practical applications for Christians. He connected his modern audience to the original readers by looking at common circumstances between both audiences. First, Israel had mourners who had to "open their heavy hearts."⁶⁴ In the same way for Christians, "No grief should unfit us for feeling thankful joy for the great common gift of 'a common salvation.'"⁶⁵ The application here is marked by a change of style from primarily using third-person pronouns to using first-person plural pronouns, as well as the appearance of the word "should" to show obligation. Second, the Israelites' booths would have been made of "miserable scrub" to remind them of the trials in the past, thus provoking them to have joy in the present. Similarly, for modern Christians, "This feast teaches that such remembrance ought always to trace the better present to God, and that memory of conquered sorrows and trials is wholesome only when it is devout, and that the joy of present ease is bracing, not when it is self-sufficient, but when it is thankful."⁶⁶ Therefore, he urged his audience to thank God because they should look at their "peace and abundance" as "God's work."⁶⁷ As shown here, the application was marked again by a change to the first-person plural pronouns, and he emphasized that God's command was meant to be impressed upon the hearts of God's people.

---

59. Maclaren, *Exodus, Leviticus and Numbers*, 261–62.
60. Maclaren, *Exodus, Leviticus and Numbers*, 262–64.
61. Maclaren, *Exodus, Leviticus and Numbers*, 264.
62. Maclaren, *Exodus, Leviticus and Numbers*, 265.
63. Maclaren, *Exodus, Leviticus and Numbers*, 265.
64. Maclaren, *Exodus, Leviticus and Numbers*, 265.
65. Maclaren, *Exodus, Leviticus and Numbers*, 266
66. Maclaren, *Exodus, Leviticus and Numbers*, 266.
67. Maclaren, *Exodus, Leviticus and Numbers*, 266.

Maclaren concluded with three passages that show how Jesus is the fulfillment of the Feast of Booths. He said that Jesus' words in John 7:37 and John 8:12 might have been recitations traditionally recited during the Feast of Booths in Jesus' time. Maclaren made this connection by looking at the Talmud and showing how its description of the Feast of Booths is similar to Christ's proclamations.[68] He admitted that "the existence of the allusion is doubtful," so he concluded with a clearer allusion in Rev 7:9.[69] The festival is a pattern for the eschatological feast where Christians will be joined with Christ. He said, "There, changeless but increasing joy will be course, and the backward look of thankful wonder will enhance the sweetness of the blessed present, and confirm the calm and sure hope of an ever-growing glory stretching shoreless and bright before us."[70] Thus, Maclaren's sermon on Lev 23:33–44 shows his method of applying Old Testament law. After explaining the text in its original context, he found the timeless truth which the law intended to teach. He then used this theological principle to apply the text to situations similar to that of the original hearers. In doing this, the law is meant to point people to Christ as the ultimate fulfillment of the law.

DISCUSSION QUESTIONS

1. Why is it better to focus on the theological principle behind a law rather than immediately relegating a law to the categories of ceremonial, political, or moral content?

2. What are some Old Testament practices, ceremonies, and objects whose purpose was fulfilled by Jesus Christ? How does Christ fulfill them?

3. Try finding text-grounded applications for Exod 23:14–11, Exod 29:19–30, and Deut 6:1–9.

---

68. Maclaren, *Exodus, Leviticus and Numbers*, 266–68
69. Maclaren, *Exodus, Leviticus and Numbers*, 268
70. Maclaren, *Exodus, Leviticus and Numbers*, 268.

4

Prayers of the Saints
The Psalms

"If the rest of Scripture may be called the speech of the Spirit of God to men, this book is the answer of the Spirit of God in men."

—Alexander Maclaren

My freshman year of college was spent at the University of Alabama. I grew up in and around Tuscaloosa, so I was excited to go to my first Alabama football game as a student. The previous year, Alabama had won a national championship, so there were high hopes for the team being able to repeat. The new team was about to be introduced when a song started playing on the loudspeakers. The song, "We are the Champions" by Queen, is a song that has been played in sports arenas for the last several decades. When the chorus struck, the crowd belted out the song, celebrating at the top of their lungs.

For about as long as humans have had writing, we have chosen to express our feelings in songs, lyrics, and poems. Many of our children's books are even written in poem form. Music and poetry touches hearts in ways that prose cannot.

The Biblical authors were no different from us today. A large portion of the Bible is written in the form of poetry and music. Textbooks on religion and theology today are written didactically and in paragraph form. But God in his infinite wisdom has chosen to teach us things about himself and ourselves using poems and music. We should be thankful that he did because some of the most memorable, quotable, and comforting passages of the Bible are not written in dry prose but as a line of a beautiful lyric. They are powerful because of that reason. God was very wise when he chose to inspire the authors to include poetry in the Bible.

Some poems exist in the New Testament epistles and Revelation. Most of the poetry in the Bible, though, is in the Old Testament, with the largest poetic book in the Bible being the book of Psalms. The book of Psalms forms a major portion of the Old Testament both in its size and function within the canon. Once you understand how the Old Testament poems work, you can easily transfer that knowledge to the New Testament poems as well.

The unique qualities of the psalms present expository preachers with numerous obstacles when crafting applications. For example, the poetry in the book of Psalms often uses poetic images to convey a point rather than clear propositions or straightforward statements. Sandy and Rata argue, "They must be read with heart and not just head." To complicate matters, the poetic verse in the psalms is different from Western poetic standards.[1] Scholars still debate the exact structure and function of Hebrew poetic parallelism.[2] This quality of Hebrew poetry makes it difficult for preachers who are accustomed to teaching propositional truths to their audience.[3] Arthurs describes the dilemma well:

> The psalms were accompanied by music. Are we supposed to sing our sermons? The psalms are personal. But how can we turn subjective experience into public address? The psalms are lyrical—full of emotion and image. How, though, can we translate high artistic language into vernacular? You can see why some preachers avoid the psalms. Their intuition tells them that we murder when we dissect.[4]

The cultural difference between the psalms and contemporary listeners is another issue that preachers face when preaching from the book. Chisholm points out,

---

1. Sandy and Rata, "Approaching the Psalms," 4; Smith, *Recapturing the Voice of God*, 126.
2. Kaiser Jr., *Toward an Exegetical Theology*, 211–12.
3. Sandy and Rata, "Approaching the Psalms," 3.
4. Arthurs, *Preaching with Variety*, 39.

> The challenge is great. As we read the psalms, we become aware of the chasm between the psalmists and us. The psalmists worshiped the one true God in a different historical-cultural context than the one in which modern Christians live. To bridge that chasm, we must have a strategy that successfully links the psalmists' horizons with our own. We must not simply describe how the psalmists spoke to God, as a history teacher might. Nor can we rip the psalms from their original context and read a meaning into them that is foreign to God's intention, for such readings lack authority. We must take seriously the meaning of the psalms in their original context and, building on this foundation, demonstrate how they are significant for us.[5]

This cultural "chasm" between the ancient authors and readers today is felt in several places. The outline and logical flow of a number of psalms can be complex and hard to follow.[6] Some of the topics in the psalms, such as the imprecatory portions which call upon God to punish his enemies, are especially difficult for Western readers to understand. The metaphors and images used by the authors often are culturally bound as well.[7]

In addition to the poetic and cultural qualities of the psalms, the Hebrew propensity to use poetry to teach theology is foreign to Western scholarship. For instance, in contrast to works on systematic or biblical theology, a psalm is not meant to be a complete theological treatise on a given subject.[8] Furthermore, the psalmists often used language with purposeful ambiguities and complexities rather than clarity.[9] For these reasons, Smith correctly states,

> [Psalms] do not take the time to tie up loose theological ends. . . . They do not fit our molds of understanding God, and they do not fit in neat homiletical forms (praise God). They are messy and difficult as the human condition. And yet, they are the perfect inspired Word of God.[10]

The lack of research on how to correctly apply the psalms is an additional, unfortunate reality for preachers. Works on interpretation and

---

5. Chisholm, Jr., "Interpreting the Psalms," 16–17.
6. Ralston, "Preaching the Psalms," 31.
7. Fee and Stuart, *How to Read the Bible for All Its Worth*, 188.
8. Smith, *Recapturing the Voice of God*, 124.
9. Sandy and Rata, "Approaching the Psalms," 4.
10. Smith, *Recapturing the Voice of God*, 123–24.

teaching the book of Psalms often speak to the complexities of Hebrew poetry, but they neglect to show how poetic verse speaks to application. Application comes more easily when the text has clear imperatives and propositional truths arranged in logical outlines. By contrast, clear application statements are not characteristic of the book of Psalms as a whole.

We need models for how to correctly apply the psalms in a way that is meaningful to the audience while conveying the authorial intent. As before, Alexander Maclaren can serve as such a model. Maclaren published more volumes on the book of Psalms than any other book of the Bible—six in total. His three-volume set in *The Expositor's Bible* has been singled out by both his peers and contemporary reviewers for its contribution to scholarship and preaching. Maclaren's applications from the psalms remained faithful to authorial intent because he grounded his applications on the theological proposition the biblical author sought to convey in the text.

HOW TO MODEL MACLAREN IN THE PSALMS

Maclaren believed the psalms comment on both the Old Testament law and the New Testament faith. The primary function of the psalms in the biblical canon was to show a faithful believer "echoing" the spirit of the law. Maclaren observed,

> The Psalter is the echo in devout hearts of the other portions of divine revelation. There are in it, indeed, further disclosures of God's mind and purposes, but its special characteristic is—the reflection of the light of God from brightened faces and believing hearts.[11]

The psalmists were hearing what God said to them in the law, applying the spirit of the law to their circumstances, and responding back to God, like an echo returning to its speaker.

However, the psalms are more than human responses and prayers to God. The authors were inspired by the Holy Spirit, and so "as we hold it to be inspired, we cannot simply say that it is man's response to God's voice. But if the rest of Scripture may be called the speech of the Spirit of God *to* men, this book is the answer of the Spirit of God *in* men."[12] Even though the book of Psalms is filled with prayers to God, it is still inspired Scripture.

---

11. Maclaren, *Psalms I to XLIX*, 1.
12. Maclaren, *Psalms I to XLIX*, 1. Emphasis original.

Maclaren also saw the psalmists' trust and devotion to God as equivalent to Christian faith. No difference existed between the two, except that in the New Testament the doctrine of faith is more fully developed.[13] Therefore, Maclaren attested that when you find the theological proposition the psalmist wished to echo, you then can show how the message and methods of the psalmist are still applicable to people today. The prayers and songs of the psalmists can be applied to Christians because of their shared faith in God, so how does one do that?

1. Understand the Content and Context of the Psalm.

To begin, make sure to explain the substance of the text, and do not neglect the larger literary and historical context in which the verses are found. Maclaren made this explicit in one sermon when he said, "So, looking not only at the words I have read, but at the whole of their setting, which is influenced by the thought of this parallelism we see here."[14] One reviewer erroneously argued that Maclaren's expositions of the psalms were not based on their historical and social background.[15] This was not the case. He explicitly revealed the historical context of numerous psalms.[16] Maclaren believed it was important to tie the explanation of the text to the literary and historical context because preachers could not properly apply the psalm without understanding the author's original intent. He declared,

> We are not to read into these words New Testament depths and fullness of meaning; we are to take them and try to find out what they meant to David and to his people; and so we shall get a firm basis for any deeper significance which we may hereafter see in them.[17]

Similarly, preachers should study the psalm itself to discover the author's setting, and then use the historical context to help explain and apply the text.[18] In other words, you must ascertain the psalm's meaning for the original readers before going to the New Testament and applying it to Christians.

13. Maclaren, *Psalms I to XLIX*, 18–19.
14. Maclaren, *Psalms LI to CXLV*, 386. Cf. Maclaren, *Psalms I to XLIX*, 130–31, 179–80, 190, 214; Maclaren, *Last Sheaves*, 92; Maclaren, *Psalms LI to CXLV*, 42–43.
15. Anonymous, "New Literature" (1909), 356.
16. Maclaren, *Christ in the Heart*, 244; Maclaren, *Psalms I to XLIX*, 2, 206–7, and 213–14.
17. Maclaren, *Psalms I to XLIX*, 113.
18. E.g. Maclaren, *Life of David*, 10; Maclaren, *Psalms I to XLIX*, 209–10.

Explanation of the text itself need not be long—sometimes only a few sentences.[19] Regularly include the significance of the important Hebrew terms in the text.[20] Most of all, make sure to reveal the emotions or "spirit" of the text to the hearers. Maclaren believed that the psalms convey the spirit of Israel's histories.[21] This spirit "breathes" from the text itself and conveys lessons about God.[22] Both the spirit and the lessons it conveys are vital to understanding the psalm itself and still are true for today's readers.[23] Therefore, preach the psalms "with the hope that we may catch something of their fervor and their glow."[24] Try to get the audience to "feel its force as the utterance of a soul seeking after and finding God."[25]

Multiple methods can be used to communicate the spirit of the psalm. In some sermons, you may point out the emotion that "throbs" from the text.[26] You can also tell your hearers to "think of the picture that rises from these graphic words"[27] Make sure your delivery itself is passionate and emotes the spirit of the text. Choules heard Maclaren preach Ps 25:14 at Southampton and voiced, "The reasoning was close and the peroration as pathetic and earnest as I can imagine to be possible."[28] Use poetic language when preaching the psalms, especially during the climactic portions of the messages. For example, Maclaren once said about Ps 1, "Though the sacred characters be but partially legible to us now, what He wrote, on stars and flowers, on the infinitely great and infinitely small, on the infinitely near and the infinitely far off, with His creating hand, was the one inscription—God is love."[29] Later in the same sermon, he said,

> Love threatens that it may never have to execute its threats. Love warns that we may be wise in time. Love prophesies that its sad forebodings may not be fulfilled. And love smites with lighter

---

19. See Maclaren, *Christ in the Heart*, 249.
20. Maclaren, *Last Sheaves*, 99; Maclaren, *Psalms I to XLIX*, 58, 164, 190, 200, 222.
21. Maclaren, *Psalms I to XLIX*, 9.
22. Maclaren, *Life of David*, 40.
23. Maclaren, *Psalms I to XLIX*, 9.
24. Maclaren, *Psalms I to XLIX*, 131.
25. Maclaren, *Christ in the Heart*, 244. Cf. Maclaren, *Psalms LI to CXLV*, 42–43.
26. Maclaren, *Psalms I to XLIX*, 113 and 195.
27. Maclaren, *Christ in the Heart*, 246.
28. Choules, *Cruise of the Steam Yacht North Star*, 67–68.
29. Maclaren, *Psalms I to XLIX*, 4.

strokes of premonitory chastisements, that we may never need to feel the whips of scorpions.[30]

Taylor argues that Maclaren naturally spoke poetically, and his natural style strengthened his preaching from the psalms.[31] Maclaren believed that helping the audience experience a psalm's emotional weight was an important part of explaining the authorial intent of the text.

2. Find the Author's Theological Lesson in the Psalm.

Once Maclaren explained the text, he gave his audience the theological proposition which the author meant to convey. Maclaren saw the psalmists as using multiple means to teach doctrine. Sometimes the words can be taken directly as theological truths.[32] At other times, the psalmists created an "image," which suggests a proposition.[33] The psalmist's experience, emotions, and response to that experience could also teach theology.[34] Maclaren explicitly stated in one sermon, "His experience may teach us the interpretation of his glad assurance."[35] Furthermore, the psalmists frequently used the poem's divisions to reinforce their main theological proposition. Likewise, divisions in one's sermon should not be random and isolated themes but instead built upon each other, further explaining the main doctrinal point of the full text.[36]

Maclaren's explanation of the text could be short at times, leaving a large portion of his main points to amplify the theological truth in the text. Maclaren saw this as explaining the "thoughts" of the psalm.[37] Maclaren did not import theological significance into a psalm but rather exegeted the psalm to discover the universal lesson the author wished to express. In like

---

30. Maclaren, *Psalms I to XLIX*, 6.

31. Taylor, "Psalms, v 1: Psalms 1–38," 496.

32. Maclaren, *Wearied Christ*, 311; Maclaren, *After the Resurrection*; 205–7, 208–9, and 211; Maclaren, *Book of Psalms I-XXXVIII*, 5–6 and 137.

33. Maclaren, *Psalms I to XLIX*, 211 and 222–23; Maclaren, *Book of Psalms XC-CL*, 160–61.

34. Maclaren, *Book of Psalms XXXIX—LXXXIX*, 234–36; Maclaren, *Secret of Power*, 234; Maclaren, *Sermons Preached in Manchester: Second Series*, 270; Maclaren, *Psalms LI to CXLV*, 41.

35. Maclaren, *Psalms I to XLIX*, 194.

36. Maclaren, *Psalms I to XLIX*, 179–85

37. Maclaren, *Psalms I to XLIX*, 31, 114, 123, 224.

manner, do not impose a doctrine onto the text. Rather, exegete the text in order to unearth the point which the author intended to convey.[38] Once you find the author's theological purpose, look to the New Testament and note how the doctrine was further developed in later revelation.[39]

Often, Maclaren signaled the psalm's theological principle by using a propositional statement in the third person. Then, he moved to first-person plural pronouns to further elaborate on this theology.[40] Instead of giving an explicit propositional statement, he also explained the psalmist's experience using broad or universal terms so that the hearers could personally identify with it.[41] In the same way, indicate to your audience that you are giving the psalmist's theological purpose by speaking in universal terms and using the first-person plural pronouns rather than referring to the original audience.

3. Look for How the Psalm Points to Jesus.

Maclaren strongly held to the need for a personal relationship with Jesus Christ. Since the theological proposition of a psalm often involves God's relationship with humanity, he used this relationship to preach about Christ from the psalms. However, like Maclaren, be careful not to impose Christ upon the text. Instead, even in clear Christological passages such as Ps 31:5, the text must first be understood in its original context before looking at how it connects to Christ.[42]

Maclaren did not believe he was imposing Christ onto a psalm when he preached about Christ because he believed the psalmists were looking to a future fulfillment.[43] Even though the psalmists did not know all the details, the New Testament reveals that the future fulfillment came with Christ.[44] Be careful, therefore, to explain the psalm and its theological proposition in its literary and historical context before including how it points to Jesus Christ.

---

38. Maclaren, *Book of Psalms XC-CL*, 160; Maclaren, *Psalms I to XLIX*, 157; cf. Maclaren, *Psalms I to XLIX*, 198, 199.

39. Maclaren, *Book of Psalms I-XXXVIII*, 139.

40. Maclaren, *Conquering Christ*, 86; Maclaren, *Psalms I to XLIX*, 200; Maclaren, *Christ in the Heart*, 245; Maclaren, *Last Sheaves*, 93; Maclaren, *Secret of Power*, 229–30; Maclaren, *Wearied Christ*, 307.

41. Maclaren, *Psalms LI to CXLV*, 388; Maclaren, *Psalms I to XLIX*, 177; Maclaren, *Christ in the Heart*, 247.

42. Maclaren, *Psalms I to XLIX*, 170–71. Cf. Maclaren, *Psalms I to XLIX*, 66–67.

43. Maclaren, *Psalms I to XLIX*, 116–19.

44. Maclaren, *Book of Psalms I-XXXVIII*, 76. Maclaren, *Psalms I to XLIX*, 225.

A wide variety of methods can be used to preach Christ from the psalms. Sometimes, the people's relationship with God during the psalmist's days is true of people with Christ now.[45] Christ is the ultimate example believers should follow when obeying the psalm.[46] Consider finding a New Testament passage demonstrating how Jesus said something similar to the psalmist's words as well.[47] Christ is our power or motivation to obey the psalm.[48] Furthermore, biblical theology also might show how Christ is the final revelation of the theology on display in the psalm.[49] However, Maclaren's most common method was to show how Christ is the ultimate source of blessing or solution that resolves the sinful problem in the text.[50] The blessings, satisfaction, or joy given to the psalmist by God is even more abundantly available to all those who have trusted in Christ.

4. Apply the Theological Lesson of the Psalm.

After he explained the psalm, gave its theological proposition, and discovered how it pointed to Christ, Maclaren applied the passage. He often changed his preaching style to mark these applications. Preachers today can mirror his approach. One can make regular use of interrogative and conditional sentences.[51] Listeners may be told they "need to," "have to," or "must" believe or do what the text confirms.[52] Use the second-person pronoun when applying the text. In fact, a direct command was Maclaren's favorite means of communicating how the text should be applied.[53] Often,

---

45. Maclaren, *Psalms I to XLIX*, 192.

46. Maclaren, *Secret of Power*, 232;.Maclaren, *Psalms I to XLIX*, 74–75, 169.

47. Maclaren, *Last Sheaves*, 102; Maclaren, *Psalms I to XLIX*, 138–39, 170.

48. Maclaren, *Conquering Christ*, 91–92.

49. Maclaren, *Psalms I to XLIX*, 67, 129–30, 189; Maclaren, *After the Resurrection*, 208–9.

50. Maclaren, *Christ in the Heart*, 254; Maclaren, *Psalms I to XLIX*, 67, 202, 225; Maclaren, *Last Sheaves*, 101–2; Maclaren, *Psalms LI to CXLV*, 46–47, 392; Maclaren, *Book of Psalms I-XXXVIII*, 75–76, 110.

51. Maclaren, *Christ in the Heart*, 246, 248, 254; Maclaren, *Psalms I to XLIX*, 179 and 193; Maclaren, *Psalms LI to CXLV*, 390; Maclaren, *Last Sheaves*, 101; Maclaren, *Psalms I to XLIX*, 170, 174, 193.

52. Maclaren, *Christ in the Heart*, 245, 249; Maclaren, *Last Sheaves*, 94; Maclaren, *Psalms I to XLIX*, 28, 192, 193, and 195; Maclaren, *Conquering Christ*, 97.

53. Maclaren, *Christ in the Heart*, 254; Maclaren, *Last Sheaves*, 97, 98; Maclaren, *Psalms I to XLIX*, 9, 94, 211; Maclaren, *Psalms LI to CXLV*, 392.

he turned the theological proposition of the text into an imperative for Christians to follow.[54]

Maclaren treated the purpose of application as to enforce the theological thoughts of the psalm upon the hearer. He told his audience in one sermon, "That is the Psalmist's teaching, and I will try to enforce it."[55] Maclaren believed since Christians share a common faith with the psalmists, then there is little need to differentiate between what the psalm meant in the past and what it means now. The psalms speak directly to "us," or all people who have received God's grace through saving faith.

Several methods can be used to find applications in a psalm. Maclaren argued that the psalms were meant to be applied to many settings regardless of the circumstances from which the psalm arose. For instance, the events which prompted the psalms are often described in general terms and were used in a worship setting apart from their historical setting.[56] Furthermore the psalmists essentially were connecting their lives to God's people in the past and then composing their works so that future saints could connect to God's people as well.[57] Maclaren, in a similar vein, applied the psalms to Christians by connecting the psalmists' experiences to comparable circumstances in his listeners' lives.

Preachers today can use the same method. Invite people to reflect on their own experiences. Maclaren noted, "The Christian experience more than repeats the psalmist's here, and the Christian hopes are at once certified and surpassed by Christ."[58] In another sermon, Maclaren told his audience to "learn, too, from this image, in which the Psalmist appropriates to himself the experience of a past generation, how we ought to feed our confidence and enlarge our hopes by all God's past dealings with men."[59] He believed that even when the psalmist did not intend a spiritual application, Christians could apply the psalm to spiritual needs since New Testament authors spiritualized the events in the psalms.[60] In general, because God does not

---

54. Maclaren, *Secret of Power*, 224–27 and 235; Maclaren, *Sermons Preached in Manchester: Second Series*, 264–65 and 271.
55. Maclaren, *Psalms I to XLIX*, 45.
56. Maclaren, *Life of David*, 9.
57. Maclaren, *Life of David*, 135.
58. Maclaren, *Last Sheaves*, 101–2.
59. Maclaren, *Psalms I to XLIX*, 211.
60. Maclaren, *Psalms LI to CXLV*, 42; Maclaren, *Book of Psalms XC-CL*, 161, 164.

change, the theological proposition of the text remains true throughout time and thus needs to be applied and appropriated by Christians.[61]

Maclaren frequently highlighted two common experiences when applying the psalms to his hearers. First, humans emotionally react to similar circumstances regardless of time, culture, or place. Therefore, the emotions or spirit of the psalm can help contemporary readers understand how the theological message of the text can be applied in their own lives. After "disengaging from the mere husk and shell of Old Testament experience," we can relate to the psalm because of the shared emotions in similar settings today.[62] Tell your audience to "picture to yourself the moment" in order to help them experience the emotional impact of the psalm.[63] Challenge people to think of their own emotional responses that prove the theological proposition of the psalm is true.[64] When doing this, make sure you preach the psalm itself and not the narrative suggested by the superscript or historical context. Maclaren focused on the text and the emotions expressed in the text and not on the historical circumstances that gave rise to the psalm.[65]

Next, like Maclaren, emphasize the continuation between how the psalmists' experienced God and how Christians experience God. Maclaren was convinced the psalmists had the same faith in God as Christians today do. The only difference was that the psalmists had not received God's full revelation. Therefore, the psalmists' devotion to God and their relationship with God can be linked to Christian faith. Maclaren argued in one sermon,

> The emotion or the act of his will and heart which he expresses in these words of my text is neither more nor less than the Christian act of faith. There is no difference except a difference of development; there is no difference between the road to God marked out in the Psalms, and the road to God laid down in the Gospels. The Psalmist who said, 'Trust ye in the Lord for ever,' and the Apostle who said, 'Believe on the Lord Jesus Christ, and thou shalt be saved,' were preaching identically the same doctrine. One of them could speak more fully than the other could of the person on whom trust was to be rested, but he trust itself was the same, and the Person on

---

61. Maclaren, *Last Sheaves*, 98, 101; Maclaren, *Psalms I to XLIX*, 214.

62. Maclaren, *Christ in the Heart*, 253–54. Cf. Maclaren, *Book of Psalms I-XXXVIII*, 119.

63. Maclaren, *Sermons Preached in Manchester: Second Series*, 268.

64. Maclaren, *Last Sheaves*, 97. Cf. Maclaren, *Psalms I to XLIX*, 8–9, 49, 215.

65. Maclaren, *Christ in the Heart*, 246.

whom it rested was the same, though His Name of old was Jehovah, and His Name to-day is 'Immanuel, God with us.'[66]

The means of approaching God is the same for New Testament believers as it was for Old Testament saints.[67] The psalms, in essence, are the prayers of faithful believers.[68] This explains why Maclaren often spoke as if a psalm was directly applicable to his church.[69] Consequently, preach the psalms as examples of how faithful Christians should respond when facing circumstances similar to what the psalmists faced.[70] Encourage people to learn or memorize the psalm and to pray after its "pattern."[71] God continues to respond to the prayers of Christians in a similar way to how he responded to the psalmists' prayers.[72]

MAIN TAKEAWAYS FROM MACLAREN FOR THE PSALMS

Preachers can still learn from Maclaren about how to apply the psalms in a way that keeps the authorial intent. Specifically, Maclaren's emphasis on theology can help with application. His sermons on the psalms contained very little explanation because he understood the text to be inherently timeless. The psalms were voices of faithful believers echoing God's revelation back to him in the form of prayers; hence, they more directly reveal theological truth than the narratives or the law. The concept of the psalms as both divine revelation and human echoes of previously canonized revelation is a homiletical compass from Maclaren that you likewise can use to connect the text to your audience.

The interaction between God and the faithful believer was Maclaren's main theological bridge to connect the text to his audience. He frequently

---

66. Maclaren, *Psalms I to XLIX*, 18–19.

67. Maclaren, *Psalms I to XLIX*, 221–22.

68. Maclaren, *Psalms I to XLIX*, 164; Maclaren, *Victory in Failure*, 128; Maclaren, *Secret of Power*, 223.

69. Maclaren, *Last Sheaves*, 92; Maclaren, *Book of Psalms I-XXXVIII*, 1–3; Maclaren, *Sermons Preached in Manchester: Second Series*, 275.

70. Maclaren, *Christ in the Heart*, 247–48; Maclaren, *Psalms I to XLIX*, 211; Maclaren, *Secret of Power*, 233; Maclaren, *Psalms LI to CXLV*, 43–44; Maclaren, *Book of Psalms XXXIX-LXXXIX*, 342–45.

71. Maclaren, *Psalms I to XLIX*, 69, 168, and 167–68; Maclaren, *Life of David*, 224; Maclaren, *Victory in Failure*, 132, 141.

72. Maclaren, *Last Sheaves*, 98.

looked to how God and his covenant people responded to each another in the psalm. Since the psalmist was a saint who had the same faith in God as New Testament Christians do in Christ, the audience can appropriate his troubles, emotions, and responses for themselves. In other words, help your audience identify with the psalmist so that they can take hold of the relevant application. Others have agreed with Maclaren that the psalms purposefully contain general language and ambiguous settings to help readers identify with the psalmists.[73] Using this principle of identification, Maclaren had two means of applying the psalms that deserve particular consideration from text-driven preachers.

1. Point out the Psalmist's Emotions and Connect Them to Today.

First, point out how the psalmists' emotions are still experienced by Christians. Psalms speak to the whole human experience, including the emotions. While they teach theological truth, preachers should not speak as if their only purpose is to grow people's theological knowledge. Psalms do more than describe; their poetry is meant to create an emotional impact. Fee and Stuart wrote this about the book of Psalms: "It is intended to appeal to the emotions, to evoke feelings rather than propositional thinking, and to stimulate a response on the part of the individual that goes beyond a mere cognitive understanding of certain facts."[74] Arthurs likewise argues, "Poetry is a language of images and emotions that the reader must experience. This is how the psalms work, and we must yield to their poetic nuances in our study."[75] Biblical poetry is often more personal than other genres, even displaying complex, contradicting, and changing emotions within a single psalm. The psalms, therefore, direct the reader toward God while not downplaying the reality of emotions such as suffering, pain, joy, or thankfulness.

Maclaren thus connected his audience to the emotions in the psalms. He not only pointed out the emotional language the psalmist was using, but he looked to the psalmist's emotions as a means of applying the text.[76] His audience might not have shared the same setting as the psalmist; however, they shared the same human emotions. He did not apply his text to

---

73. Doriani, *Getting the Message*, 239–40; Smith, *Recapturing the Voice of God*, 123.
74. Fee and Stuart, *How to Read the Bible for All Its Worth*, 190.
75. Arthurs, *Preaching with Variety*, 49.
76. Maclaren, *Victory in Failure*, 132–34.

situations that were dissimilar to the original context but instead looked for situations in his day that elicited the same emotions from his hearers that the psalmist felt. Therefore, your sermon also ought to demonstrate how emotions relate to one's relationship with God. Acknowledge that feelings are common when God's people relate Scripture to the world around them. Invite your hearers to remember times when they felt the same emotions as the psalmist. In return, the audience can be invited to express their emotions and burdens to God in manners similar to the psalmists.[77]

2. Give an Appropriate Response to God.

Psalms still function today as they did then: prayers of God's people to God. Smith said, "The psalms do not provide a license to whine; they are instead a promise of hope. They give voice to our quests about justice."[78] Psalms teach how people should worship, pray, and approach God. They portray how humans can respond rightly and honestly to God, especially through prayer and worship, and they are meant to deepen both public and private worship. The psalms, then, are divinely sanctioned examples that show future believers how to respond to God.

Maclaren repeatedly showed how the psalmists' responses to God are the appropriate responses in a given situation for all time. Sometimes, Maclaren applied the text by telling his audience to emulate the psalmist. At other times, he changed the theological proposition of the text into an imperative which Christians ought to obey. However, outside of the imprecations, he especially looked to the psalmists as examples of how Christians should correctly respond to God through prayer and worship. Similarly, when applying the psalms, you can challenge your hearers to use the psalm as a map to express their emotions and burdens to God in prayer. The variety in the psalms is especially useful. A psalm may demonstrate a habit for praying or worshipping which your audience might not have considered before. Therefore, use the psalm as a model to teach how to worship and pray.

Maclaren can serve as a model for preachers seeking to apply the psalms. He believed the psalmists' responses to God were not simply human words but an inspired word from God. Maclaren connected his audience to the book of Psalms by finding the author's theological purpose for

---

77. Kaiser Jr., *Preaching and Teaching from the Old Testament*, 126; Doriani, *Getting the Message*, 242.

78. Smith, *Recapturing the Voice of God*, 136.

writing the psalms. Consequently, he urged his audience to emulate both the psalmists' prayers and how they relate to God. Look to Maclaren to better learn how to use both the psalmists' emotions and their responses to God to apply the book of Psalms to new covenant believers.

SERMON BREAKDOWN: "SEEKING THE FACE OF GOD"

Maclaren's sermon "Seeking the Face of God" from Ps 27:8–9 is a good example of his preaching from the book of Psalms for several reasons. First, both the structure of his sermon as a whole and each main point are characteristic of the majority of his sermon structures on the Psalms. Second, the stylistic features of the sermon, such as moments of poetic language, are similar to what he demonstrated frequently when preaching the psalms. Lastly, his applications in this sermon perfectly illustrate his homiletical practice when applying the psalms. For these reasons, "Seeking the Face of God" provides a case study of his methodology when preaching from the book of Psalms.

Maclaren began by discussing the larger historical and literary context of Ps 27 in the introduction of his sermon. He accepted the author as David and mined the literary context to discover the circumstances that led David to pen this psalm. Summing up the psalm's overall message, he connected the poem's lines to potential moments in David's past such as the slaying of Goliath. The psalmist's theological understanding of the past became the "piers of an arch" from which he prayed the words of the psalm.[79] He saw the psalmist as reiterating divine truth stated elsewhere in Scripture.

Maclaren's main points were stated as phrases rather than full propositions. Like many of his sermons on the psalms, he conveyed the "thoughts" in the text using phrases rather than sentences. He announced the first by saying, "There is here, first, God's voice to the heart."[80] After explaining how his first and second main points relate, he invited his audience to "observe a little more closely what the Psalmist means by the phrase 'seeking God's face.'"[81]

He spent several paragraphs describing the theological meaning of the phrase "seeking God's face." His comments were not a digression from the text because Maclaren believed the psalmist meant for his readers to recall the full theological force of the phrase "seeking God's face." God does not

---

79. Maclaren, *Secret of Power*, 222.
80. Maclaren, *Secret of Power*, 224.
81. Maclaren, *Secret of Power*, 224.

have a literal face, Maclaren argued, but chose to describe himself this way to facilitate man's understanding of his character. He defined the face of God as "that aspect or side of the divine nature which is turned to man, and is perceptible to him."[82] The psalmist used "the face of God" both to picture God's "dazzling brightness" and "the knowable part of the Divine nature."[83] The phrase prevents the reader from falling into theological error, or as Maclaren put it, "keeps us from the twin errors of supposing that we can know nothing of God, and of forgetting that we can know but an aspect and a side of His nature."[84] Maclaren concluded that "to seek God's face is no long, dubious search, nor is He hard to be found. We have only to desire to possess—and to act in harmony with the desire—and we shall walk all the day in the light of His countenance."[85] This is the theological proposition the author meant to convey by the phrase "seeking God's face."

Now, Maclaren turned this theological truth into an application for his listeners. Imperative sentences and second-person pronouns signal his application of the text. By way of example, he said, "Endeavor to keep vivid the consciousness of that face as looking always in on you," and "scrupulously avoid whatever might dim the vision of His face."[86] He contended that the invitation to seek God's face is extended to every individual. This exhortation led to the poetic climax for his first main point:

> By the very make of our spirits, which bear on them alike in their weakness and their strength the sign that they are His, and can only be at rest in Him, He says, "Seek ye my face." By all His providences of joy or sorrow, by disappointments and fulfilments, by hopes and fruitions, by losses and gains, by all the alternations which "toss us to His breast," He says, "Seek ye my face."[87]

He ended this first main point by discussing how the text ultimately is fulfilled in Jesus' person and teachings. Jesus is the "true 'angel of His face,' in whom all the lustre of His radiance is gathered." Jesus calls people, therefore, to "come unto me, all ye that labour and are heaven laden."[88]

---

82. Maclaren, *Secret of Power*, 225.
83. Maclaren, *Secret of Power*, 225.
84. Maclaren, *Secret of Power*, 226.
85. Maclaren, *Secret of Power*, 227.
86. Maclaren, *Secret of Power*, 227–28.
87. Maclaren, *Secret of Power*, 228–29.
88. Maclaren, *Secret of Power*, 229.

Maclaren moved to his next main point by saying, "We have here the heart's echo to the voice of God."[89] He stated one sentence of explanation before giving the theological lesson, which he found in the psalmist's response toward God "as the thunder to the lightning."[90] After contrasting the psalmist's immediate response to God to the slow response of the people in Maclaren's day, he detailed the dangers of delaying one's response to God. A brief application followed naturally from these conclusions: "So do not let us tolerate any lingering hesitation in ourselves in yielding to the Divine summons."[91] Maclaren urged his audience to be like the psalmist in how he responded to God.

The response should not only immediate but also a "complete correspondence," according to Maclaren.[92] He compared the second phrase "Thy face will I seek" to the phrase discussed in the first part and pictured the psalmist as a sailor repeating the commands of his captain as he steers a ship. From this explanation, he discovered the theological proposition that "the correspondence in the words means the correspondence in action and the thorough-going obedience."[93] Once again, he contrasted how the psalmist responded to God with how many Christians in his day acted.[94]

This second sub-point was followed by a third: the response is "firm and decisive."[95] Maclaren reached this conclusion based on an exegesis of the Hebrew text. The author purposefully used only three Hebrew words. This brief response is the appropriate echo to God's voice. Maclaren expressed the theological truth in a short, compact sentence—"Fixed resolves need short professions"—and again described how many people in his day do not respond to God in this way.[96]

He then added a fourth sub-point: the personal nature of God's invitation. Pointing to the first-person singular pronouns in the text, he insisted, "That is what we have all to do with God's words. He sows His invitations broadcast: we have to make them our own."[97] After giving a few

---

89. Maclaren, *Secret of Power*, 229.
90. Maclaren, *Secret of Power*, 229.
91. Maclaren, *Secret of Power*, 230.
92. Maclaren, *Secret of Power*, 230.
93. Maclaren, *Secret of Power*, 230.
94. Maclaren, *Secret of Power*, 230–31.
95. Maclaren, *Secret of Power*, 231.
96. Maclaren, *Secret of Power*, 231.
97. Maclaren, *Secret of Power*, 232.

more examples, he connected the text to Christ, arguing that "Christ died for the world," but Christ's death is not applied until a person appropriates the death to themselves by "a personal response to it."[98] Joy comes from understanding that God speaks to us individually through his Word and sometimes through nature as well. He concluded with a one-sentence application expressed as his own, personal resolve: "Thou dost call, and I answer, Lo! here [sic] am I."[99]

He began his final main point, saying, "The heart's cry to God [is] founded on both the Divine voice and the human echo."[100] He compared the last half of the text with the first and found two theological truths are the grounds for the psalmist's prayer. First, God does not command something which He will not fulfill, so "if He bids us seek His face, He thereby pledges Himself to show us His face."[101] Second, and similarly, believers can seek God with confidence knowing that if they seek him, they will find him.

The sermon concluded with an urgent appeal. Christians ought to be motivated to seek God today for the same theological reasons that drove the psalmist to seek God back then. Thus, "'seek His face evermore,' and your life will be bright because you will walk in the light of His countenance always."[102]

DISCUSSION QUESTIONS

1. Why do songs and poems speak to us differently than prose? What is the significance, then, that God included songs and poems in Scripture?

2. In a sermon, what can you do to convey the emotions of a psalms and not merely its content?

3. Try finding text-grounded applications for Ps 1, Ps 3, and Ps 150.

---

98. Maclaren, *Secret of Power*, 232.
99. Maclaren, *Secret of Power*, 233.
100. Maclaren, *Secret of Power*, 233.
101. Maclaren, *Secret of Power*, 234.
102. Maclaren, *Secret of Power*, 235.

5

Proper Living
Wisdom Literature

"Take heed that we listen now to the beseeching call of the heavenly Wisdom in its tenderest and noblest form, as it appeared in Christ, the Incarnate Word."

—ALEXANDER MACLAREN

THE WISDOM LITERATURE SHARES several characteristics in common with the book of Psalms; thus, it seems appropriate to look now at the wisdom literature. In one Greek myth, a boy named Icarus is given wax wings by his father, who is a famous inventor. His father's one rule for Icarus was the boy should not fly too close to the sun. Unfortunately, Icarus did not believe he needed to heed his father's rule. He flew too close to the sun, his wings melted, and the boy fell to his death.

We can be like Icarus and want to fly too close to sin. We can think we know more or can do more without getting hurt than we actually can. Many of us are able to testify today that we know what it feels like to fly too close to sin, to have our metaphorical wings melt, and to plummet to earth. For this reason, God has given us an immensely valuable part of Scripture called the wisdom literature.

It should encourage you to learn that you do not have to buy a bunch of books off the internet or from a store to gain good wisdom. There are books of practical wisdom right in your Bible. The wisdom portions of Scripture help us know how to navigate life more easily and with fewer mistakes. Smith argues that what separates wisdom from the other biblical genres is "their proverbial way of leading us along on our journey. Unlike the direct commands of the Old Testament and the imperatives built on the theology of the New Testament, the Wisdom literature serves as a traveler's guide to life."[1] The biblical authors are describing someone who is skilled at living according to God's Word and is applying the Bible to everyday life. Wisdom is found throughout the New Testament, especially in the book of James. Nevertheless, the majority of wisdom passages come from four Old Testament books: Job, Proverbs, Ecclesiastes, and Song of Solomon.

Despite these books being some of the most practical portions of Scripture, they are also some of the most neglected. The preacher or teacher faces numerous obstacles when dealing with biblical wisdom. Most is written in a lyrical form, so the pastor must wrestle with the difficulties of Hebrew poetry. Furthermore, text-driven preaching follows the structure of the text, but the overall structures of the wisdom books are hard to outline. The wisdom books also seem to emphasize morals over theological reflection and the gospel. Block writes,

> How shall we understand the apparent secularity of many wisdom texts? Why are they so oblivious to the basic redemptive story line of the Bible? Wherein does their authority lie? How shall I interpret the strange figures of speech? How do I account for their resemblances to extra-biblical writings? Questions like these present unique challenges for preaching from these texts.[2]

Despite the difficulties in preaching the wisdom literature, Kaiser rightly argues, "People long for help with the basic and mundane issues of life, and preaching on each of the wisdom books can supply their hunger beyond their wildest imaginations."[3]

Preachers need a model to understand how to apply biblical wisdom appropriately. Alexander Maclaren fills this need because he exegeted his text in its original context in order to discover the theological proposition the author intended to convey. He then considered the placement of the wisdom books within progressive revelation. This helped him apply his text to his audience in a way that did justice to its original setting and was

---

1. Smith, *Recapturing the Voice of God*, 146.
2. Block, "'That They May All Fear Me,'" 68.
3. Kaiser Jr., *Preaching and Teaching from the Old Testament*, 99.

meaningful to his Christian audience. Since no sermons can be found from Maclaren on the Song of Solomon, this chapter will focus on his sermons from the books of Job, Proverbs, and Ecclesiastes to determine in what ways Maclaren models for preachers how to apply the wisdom literature.

HOW TO MODEL MACLAREN IN THE WISDOM

For Maclaren, biblical wisdom was more than intellectual knowledge or capability. Biblical wisdom involves having a proper understanding of the doctrines of Scripture and then allowing proper doctrine to undergird the person's morality and behavior.[4] Consequently, folly or foolishness, from a biblical perspective, does not mean unintelligent but "moral and religious obliquity, which are the stupidest things that a man can be guilty of."[5] In one sermon he preached, "In whatever directions a godless man may be wise, in the most important matter of all, his relations to God, he is unwise, and the epitaph for all such is 'Thou fool!'"[6] One's relationship to God is vital, so people must seek God in order to acquire wisdom.[7] Wisdom is impossible to obtain on one's own power.

This God-centered view of wisdom influenced the way Maclaren approached biblical wisdom. For him, Proverbs pictures a life lived wisely in accordance to God, showing how the fear of God brings true wisdom.[8] By contrast, Job and Ecclesiastes describe humanity in the search for true wisdom. Maclaren believed much of the books of Job and Ecclesiastes depicted partial truths derived from worldly wisdom. The complete truth is revealed at the conclusion of each book as well as in the New Testament. Job and Ecclesiastes, therefore, depict a wrestling match between wisdom derived solely from human observation and a wisdom from the heavenly God. Regardless of which wisdom book his text was found, Maclaren's sermons tended to follow a certain pattern which preachers today can emulate.

---

4. Maclaren, *Sermons Preached in Manchester: First Series*, 299.

5. Maclaren, *Esther, Job, Proverbs and Ecclesiastes*, 279.

6. Maclaren, *Esther, Job, Proverbs and Ecclesiastes*, 74; Cf. Maclaren, *Esther, Job, Proverbs and Ecclesiastes*, 204–5, 279.

7. Maclaren, *Sermons Preached in Manchester: First Series*, 300; Maclaren, *Esther, Job, Proverbs and Ecclesiastes*, 74.

8. Maclaren, *Esther, Job, Proverbs and Ecclesiastes*, 204–5.

1. Understand the Content of the Wisdom Passage.

Even though Maclaren usually preached from one or two verses when in the wisdom literature, he always considered the larger literary and historical context of his passage. Like Maclaren, make sure to study the literary and historical context when exegeting and applying a wisdom text as well.[9] Point out instances where the cultural background of the book helps explain the purpose of the text.[10] Rather than only doing topical discussions from the book of Proverbs, Maclaren sometimes took multiple consecutive proverbs as his sermon text, especially if he thought there was "a slight thread of connection" between the verses.[11] This alternative to preaching the book of Proverbs would be a refreshing change for preachers and teachers who have only attempted a topical approach to the proverbial sayings.

Once Maclaren determined the significance of the literary and historical context, he explained the meaning of his text to his audience. His explanations could be short when preaching a wisdom text because he saw the wisdom literature as teaching theological truth more directly than other biblical genres.[12] However, he was careful to reveal nuances in the Hebrew language if they helped the reader understand the text.[13] He also frequently illustrated the passage vividly as if it was a short story.[14] He helped his audience picture in their minds the scene that his text conveyed.[15] Similarly, you should help your audience understand the text by crafting illustrations and metaphors that explain and connect the text to today.

2. Find the Author's Theological Lesson in the Wisdom Passage.

After explaining the text, tell your audience the theological point the author meant to convey. Maclaren held that God was the center of the wisdom

---

9. Maclaren, *Sermons Preached in Manchester: First Series*, 294–95, 298–99; Maclaren, *Esther, Job, Proverbs and Ecclesiastes*, 29, 33–34, 298–99.

10. Maclaren, *Esther, Job, Proverbs and Ecclesiastes*, 288–89.

11. Maclaren, *Leaves from the Tree of Life*, 268; Maclaren, *Esther, Job, Proverbs and Ecclesiastes*, 155–63, 204–10, 220–221.

12. Maclaren, *Esther, Job, Proverbs and Ecclesiastes*, 30–31.

13. Maclaren, *Esther, Job, Proverbs and Ecclesiastes*, 137, 257, 290–291; Maclaren, *Leaves from the Tree of Life*, 270, 272.

14. Maclaren, *Sermons Preached in Manchester: First Series*, 302–3; Maclaren, *Esther, Job, Proverbs and Ecclesiastes*, 256–57, 280, 292–93.

15. Maclaren, *Esther, Job, Proverbs and Ecclesiastes*, 243, 281, 286.

literature. The writers might not have had specific doctrines in mind when they wrote their text; however, their texts are written within a biblical worldview.[16] The wisdom writers did not see human experiences as a result of chance but as a product of God's activity in the world.[17] Furthermore, those who seek and obey wisdom come to possess God and be filled by him.[18] Since the biblical writers were looking at human life through the lens of an almighty God, wisdom literature taught theological principles that are still true in the lives of Christians today.[19]

In order to prove the truthfulness of the text to Christians, invite audiences to see how the theological truth is demonstrated in their own lives. Maclaren called his audience to picture someone they know who was not following the wisdom in the text, and he asked his hearers to see the result of such a lifestyle.[20] Otherwise, he told the audience to look back and see how their own life experiences prove the wisdom passage is true.[21] The rest of Scripture, for the most part, taught the same principles reflected by the wisdom writers.[22] Therefore, Maclaren saw few differences between the original wisdom readers and the people in his church.

His sermons from Ecclesiastes and Job sometimes showed one distinction that was unique from Proverbs. Maclaren argued both the speeches by Job's friends and the initial chapters of Ecclesiastes contained partial or incomplete truths.[23] This incompleteness did not make these portions less inspired and inerrant than the rest of Scripture; rather, the reader only received half the story from these texts. The wisdom in these texts reflects the limited, earthly point-of-view of the characters in those chapters. But the full truth is revealed at the end of the books and ultimately with the New Testament.[24]

---

16. Maclaren, *Esther, Job, Proverbs and Ecclesiastes*, 164.
17. Maclaren, *Esther, Job, Proverbs and Ecclesiastes*, 210.
18. Maclaren, *Esther, Job, Proverbs and Ecclesiastes*, 131.
19. Maclaren, *Esther, Job, Proverbs and Ecclesiastes*, 227, 231.
20. Maclaren, *Sermons Preached in Manchester: First Series*, 296–97.
21. Maclaren, *Esther, Job, Proverbs and Ecclesiastes*, 238, 271, 284; Maclaren, *Leaves from the Tree of Life*, 273.
22. Maclaren, *Esther, Job, Proverbs and Ecclesiastes*, 291.
23. E.g. Maclaren, *Esther, Job, Proverbs and Ecclesiastes*, 54, 298.
24. Maclaren, *Esther, Job, Proverbs and Ecclesiastes*, 298, 299–301, 307.

Maclaren voiced that the book of Job more specifically dealt with the meaning of sorrow.[25] So, Job's friends make theological statements about sorrow that appear true and wise if one's view is "fixed on earth."[26] They have observed the world and concluded that suffering is linked to sin, and while this wisdom might be true sometimes, Maclaren pointed out, "These friends of Job's all err in believing that suffering is always and only the measure of sin, and that you can tell a man's great guilt by observing his great sorrows."[27] The speeches made by Job's friend thus contain "partial truth in them" but not the complete truth, as Maclaren contended,

> The close of the Book of Job shows that his friends' speeches were defective, and in part erroneous. They all proceeded on the assumption that suffering was the fruit of sin—a principle which, though true in general, is not to be unconditionally applied to specific cases. They all forgot that good men might be exposed to it, not as punishment, nor even as correction, but as trial, to 'know what was in their hearts.'[28]

The preacher must go to the New Testament to complete the theological truth in the Job's friends' speeches.[29]

Maclaren held to a similar view of Ecclesiastes. He reasoned this book was the diary of "The Preacher" and revealed his spiritual journey to godly wisdom:

> The Book of Ecclesiastes is the log-book of a voyager after the truth, and tells us all the wanderings and errors of his thinking until he has arrived at the haven of the conclusion that he announces in the final word: 'Hear the sum of the whole matter: Fear God, and keep His commandments, for this is the whole duty of man.'[30]

Since Ecclesiastes depicts a progression in spiritual thought, some of the author's words early in the book reflect thoughts the author no longer holds by the end of his journey. Maclaren went so far as to say, "Whatever may be thought of teaching on that subject which appears in the formal conclusion

---

25. Maclaren, *Esther, Job, Proverbs and Ecclesiastes*, 29.
26. Maclaren, *Esther, Job, Proverbs and Ecclesiastes*, 40.
27. Maclaren, *Esther, Job, Proverbs and Ecclesiastes*, 47.
28. Maclaren, *Esther, Job, Proverbs and Ecclesiastes*, 33. Cf. Maclaren, *Esther, Job, Proverbs and Ecclesiastes*, 35 and 40.
29. Maclaren, *Esther, Job, Proverbs and Ecclesiastes*, 33.
30. Maclaren, *Esther, Job, Proverbs and Ecclesiastes*, 323.

of the book, the belief in a future state certainly exercises no influence on its earlier portions. These represent phases through which the writer passes on his way to his conclusion."[31] From the start, "The Preacher" is "bitter" and "melancholy" because he is only seeing the world from a human point of view; they do not reflect the full theological truths revealed in the book's conclusion and in the New Testament.[32] The New Testament does not correct the theology in Ecclesiastes but complements and completes it.[33] Maclaren claimed:

> He immediately proceeds to draw from this undeniable, but, as I maintain, partial fact, the broad conclusions which cannot be rebutted, if you accept what he has said in my text as being the sufficient and complete account of man and his dwelling place . . . There is more to be said; the sad, superficial teaching of the Preacher needs to be supplemented. Now turn for a moment to what does supplement it.[34]

When studying his sermons on Job and Ecclesiastes, you must keep in mind that Maclaren believed the authors preserved these "partial truths" in order to point their readers elsewhere for the true answers. Otherwise, one can easily misread his sermons as arguing the texts do not conform to the doctrine of inerrancy.

3. Look for How the Wisdom Passage Points to Jesus.

In addition to preaching the theological proposition of the text, Maclaren frequently showed how the passage spoke of Christ. He was unsure if the biblical authors fully grasped how wisdom was connected to a future Messiah.[35] However, progressive revelation shows wisdom is not a mere attribute of God but rather a person of the godhead, namely Jesus Christ.[36] To walk in wisdom, one must

---

31. Maclaren, *Esther, Job, Proverbs and Ecclesiastes*, 316; Cf. Maclaren, *Esther, Job, Proverbs and Ecclesiastes*, 298, 318.
32. Maclaren, *Esther, Job, Proverbs and Ecclesiastes*, 298, 309, 310, 317.
33. Maclaren, *Esther, Job, Proverbs and Ecclesiastes*, 302, 308, 312.
34. Maclaren, *Esther, Job, Proverbs and Ecclesiastes*, 300–301.
35. Maclaren, *Sermons Preached in Manchester: First Series*, 301; Maclaren, *Esther, Job, Proverbs and Ecclesiastes*, 78.
36. Maclaren, *Esther, Job, Proverbs and Ecclesiastes*, 139–43.

Let the Christ who is not only wise, but Wisdom, choose your path, and be sure that by the submission of your will all your paths are His, and not only yours. Make His path yours by following in His steps, and do in your place what you think Christ would have done if He had been there. Keep company with Him on the road.[37]

Sometimes, Christ taught the same theological lesson revealed in a wisdom text.[38] Christ also can be the solution or answer to the problem presented in the text.[39] Moreover, Christ is God's ultimate revelation of the doctrine revealed in the wisdom text.[40] Maclaren's most frequent method of connecting to Christ, though, was to urge his people to seek and obey Christ. Maclaren affirmed that fear God in the Old Testament is the same as living for Christ in the New Testament. Thus, "a solemn appeal to 'be in the fear of the Lord all the day long,' which being turned into Christian language, is to live by habitual faith, in communion with, and love and obedience to, our Lord and Saviour Jesus Christ."[41] To live wisely was to have a faith that follows Christ as Lord, and the ultimate application of wisdom is to seek Christ by faith.[42] As Maclaren said, "The only complete peace, which fills and quiets the whole man, comes from obeying Wisdom, or what is the same thing, from following Christ."[43] Maclaren shows how preaching from wisdom text can be filled with evangelistic appeals.

4. Apply the Theological Lesson of the Wisdom Passage.

After explaining the text and its theological message, Maclaren applied the text to his audience. He had no problem demonstrating the relevance of his passage to his hearers because he insisted people in all ages struggle with the

---

37. Maclaren, *Esther, Job, Proverbs and Ecclesiastes*, 102. Cf. Maclaren, *Sermons Preached in Manchester: First Series*, 301; Maclaren, *Esther, Job, Proverbs and Ecclesiastes*, 51–52, 78, 82.

38. Maclaren, *Leaves from the Tree of Life*, 275; Maclaren, *Esther, Job, Proverbs and Ecclesiastes*, 30, 52, 213, 285.

39. Maclaren, *Esther, Job, Proverbs and Ecclesiastes*, 43, 130, 195, 315.

40. Maclaren, *Leaves from the Tree of Life*, 269; Maclaren, *Esther, Job, Proverbs and Ecclesiastes*, 247.

41. Maclaren, *Esther, Job, Proverbs and Ecclesiastes*, 254. Cf. Maclaren, *Esther, Job, Proverbs and Ecclesiastes*, 73.

42. Maclaren, *Sermons Preached in Manchester: First Series*, 301 and 305; Maclaren, *Esther, Job, Proverbs and Ecclesiastes*, 93, 195, 315–16.

43. Maclaren, *Esther, Job, Proverbs and Ecclesiastes*, 93.

same sinful temptations addressed in the wisdom literature.[44] He asserted, "The essentials of moral character are substantially the same in all ages."[45] The morals taught in the wisdom literature therefore changed very little after Christ came. On the contrary, "the gospel has, no doubt, raised the standard of morals, and, in many respects, altered the conception and perspective of virtues; but its great distinction lies, not so much in the novelty of its commandments as in the new motives and power to obey them."[46] Scripture directs the "highest regions of human life," so it easily has the authority to "regulate the motions of its lower phases" of moral living.[47]

Maclaren had a unique vision of what application from the wisdom literature should accomplish. Wisdom texts teach a theological principle that shines like a lamp. The job of the preacher is to flash the lamp's rays upon different spheres of life and show the practical ways the wisdom text should be applied.[48] In one sermon, Maclaren said about wisdom,

> If we would take this thought . . . and apply it directly to our own personal experience and thoughts of ourselves, we should find that, like every other commonplace of morality and religion, the apparently toothless generality has sharp enough teeth, and that the trite truth flashes up into strange beauty, and has power to purify and guide our lives.[49]

Like Maclaren, find where the theological truth is practically applicable today and then urge people to apply the clear message of the text to their own lives. By way of an example, Maclaren once preached, "The lesson it conveys is the same—the old, old lesson, so threadbare that I should be almost ashamed of taking up your time with it unless I believed that you did not lay it to your heart as you should."[50] He did not hesitate to apply a wisdom text directly to his audience.

Maclaren's applications followed several patterns when in the wisdom literature which preachers would do well to consider and emulate these patterns. For one, turn the theological proposition into a command that the people ought to follow, or apply the text with a conditional sentence. If your

---

44. Maclaren, *Esther, Job, Proverbs and Ecclesiastes*, 221–22, 263, 271, 294.
45. Maclaren, *Esther, Job, Proverbs and Ecclesiastes*, 240.
46. Maclaren, *Esther, Job, Proverbs and Ecclesiastes*, 240.
47. Maclaren, *Esther, Job, Proverbs and Ecclesiastes*, 226.
48. Maclaren, *Esther, Job, Proverbs and Ecclesiastes*, 202–4, 232.
49. Maclaren, *Esther, Job, Proverbs and Ecclesiastes*, 196–97.
50. Maclaren, *Esther, Job, Proverbs and Ecclesiastes*, 231.

hearers obeyed the text, then they would find the text's words to be true.[51] Urge listeners to hear and memorize the wisdom in the text.[52] Maclaren frequently announced, "I beseech you" before an application to enhance the urgency of his appeal.[53] Consider directing these applications toward young adults, especially when preaching on Proverbs and Ecclesiastes.[54] Moreover, as discussed above, Maclaren repeatedly compared his text with a New Testament passage that taught the same doctrine. The New Testament, and especially words spoken by Christ, can show how the wisdom text applies to Christians.[55] Finally, call upon hearers to seek and obey Christ. Since Christ is connected to God's wisdom, an appeal to follow Christ ought to become a major application of the sermon.[56] Maclaren used these methods of application regardless from which wisdom book he preached.

Maclaren showed some variety in his applications depending on whether he was preaching from Proverbs, Ecclesiastes, or Job. When preaching from the book of Proverbs, he sometimes spoke as if his text was directly applicable to his audience. He did not give long applications; instead, he asserted the theological proposition and urged his hearers to understand, believe, and follow the wisdom in their own lives.[57] If the immediate application of the text addressed a very specific issue, he expanded the application to other physical or spiritual areas of life.[58] He reasoned such a homiletical move is warranted because biblical wisdom taught universal patterns that could appear in other areas of life.[59] The proverbs already are written as universal applications from God's revelation; therefore, preachers and teachers today ought to encourage their churches to heed the proverbs like Maclaren did.

---

51. Maclaren, *Leaves from the Tree of Life*, 271; Maclaren, *Esther, Job, Proverbs and Ecclesiastes*, 81, 83, 203, 322; Maclaren, *Sermons Preached in Manchester: First Series*, 300.

52. Maclaren, *Sermons Preached in Manchester: First Series*, 297, 303; Maclaren, *Esther, Job, Proverbs and Ecclesiastes*, 215, 273, 287, 320.

53. Maclaren, *Esther, Job, Proverbs and Ecclesiastes*, 227, 229, 285, 332. Maclaren, *Sermons Preached in Manchester: First Series*, 306.

54. Maclaren, *Sermons Preached in Manchester: First Series*, 294; Maclaren, *Esther, Job, Proverbs and Ecclesiastes*, 71, 215, 247, 295, 324.

55. Maclaren, *Esther, Job, Proverbs and Ecclesiastes*, 191–95, 230, 285.

56. Maclaren, *Sermons Preached in Manchester: First Series*, 305; Maclaren, *Esther, Job, Proverbs and Ecclesiastes*, 83, 186, 234, 278, 315, 332–33.

57. E.g. Maclaren, *Esther, Job, Proverbs and Ecclesiastes*, 80.

58. Maclaren, *Esther, Job, Proverbs and Ecclesiastes*, 223–24, 269–74.

59. E.g. Maclaren, *Esther, Job, Proverbs and Ecclesiastes*, 294.

Proper Living

Maclaren took a different route when applying a text from Ecclesiastes. Even though he held that the author's initial conclusions are incomplete, he still believed they held some truth and could be applied cautiously. For example, he announced in one Ecclesiastes sermon, "Well that is not true altogether, but though it be not true altogether . . . yet the thought itself is one that has a great deal in it that is true and important, and may be very helpful and profitable to us now."[60] He believed much of Ecclesiastes needed the New Testament to be applied fully, so his applications often came at the end of his sermons after exegeting a corresponding New Testament passage. These "practical lessons" are what Christians should do once they have heard the words of both Ecclesiastes and the New Testament.[61] Consequently, his method of applying Ecclesiastes was tied to his view of the book's overall message and structure.

His applications in Job were likewise affected by his view of the book's overall theme and structure. First, Maclaren did not shy away from applying the speeches made by Job's friends to his church. When taken as they are, he said they "may rebuke and stimulate and encourage us to make our lives conformed to the ideal here."[62] Furthermore, when what they say about God is true, "we have to learn the hard lesson" of the text.[63] Nevertheless, Job's friends only describe partial truths about God and suffering. Maclaren therefore told his audience the speeches may not be true on earth like the speaker originally meant, but they may be true in the realm of eternity. They can be "raised to a higher level than that on which he placed them, and regarded as describing the sweet and wonderful prerogatives of the devout life."[64] In another sermon on one of Job's friends, he commented,

> Yet even for those who find all at once that the herd is cut off from the stall, their tabernacle may still be in peace, and though the fold be empty they may miss nothing, if in the empty place they find God. That is what Christians may make out of the words; but it is not what was originally meant by them.[65]

---

60. Maclaren, *Esther, Job, Proverbs and Ecclesiastes*, 308; Cf. Maclaren, *Esther, Job, Proverbs and Ecclesiastes*, 311–12.

61. Maclaren, *Esther, Job, Proverbs and Ecclesiastes*, 305–6, 308.

62. Maclaren, *Esther, Job, Proverbs and Ecclesiastes*, 54.

63. Maclaren, *Esther, Job, Proverbs and Ecclesiastes*, 31.

64. Maclaren, *Esther, Job, Proverbs and Ecclesiastes*, 54.

65. Maclaren, *Esther, Job, Proverbs and Ecclesiastes*, 37–38. Cf. Maclaren, *Esther, Job, Proverbs and Ecclesiastes*, 39.

The speeches can be applied in this way because many of the questions raised by the book of Job find their solution in eternity.[66] Second, not only the friends' words but also their actions can be applied.[67] The friends illustrate insufficient comforters or counselors and thus serve as negative examples of what Christians should not do when they approach someone who is suffering. In this way, Maclaren applied the wisdom text in accordance with his overall interpretation of each wisdom book.

MAIN TAKEAWAYS FROM MACLAREN FOR WISDOM

Even if one does not agree with Maclaren's conclusions regarding the overall nature of the wisdom books, his sermons still provide helpful suggestions on how to teach the texts. Preachers and teachers can follow his method in their own applications in several ways.

1. Be God-Centered in Your Applications.

Applications need to be theocentric. While theology may come naturally in other genres, the pragmatic themes of the wisdom literature make the theological nature of wisdom not so obvious. Nevertheless, numerous scholars have noted wisdom provides not only practical words for life but also truths about the person and works of God.[68] Biblical wisdom is humankind's rational observations on experiences through the lens of God's sovereignty and revelation. Furthermore, purely human wisdom is weak and faulty compared to the true wisdom that is grounded in God. As a result, the main theme of the wisdom literature is the declaration that true wisdom is only found in God.

Maclaren agreed, saying, "They got it from thinking over the facts of this present life as they appeared to them, looked at from the standpoint of a belief in God, and in righteousness."[69] He treated wisdom literature as not simply advice for wise living but as intrinsically linked to the person of God and his will for human behavior. This is why, after exegeting the text, Maclaren told his audience the theological message the text conveyed. His

---

66. Maclaren, *Esther, Job, Proverbs and Ecclesiastes*, 45.
67. Maclaren, *Esther, Job, Proverbs and Ecclesiastes*, 38, 39–40.
68. E.g. Smith, *Recapturing the Voice of God*, 146–47.
69. Maclaren, *Esther, Job, Proverbs and Ecclesiastes*, 249.

applications were built upon the foundation that biblical wisdom is theological as much as it is practical.

Similarly, put God at the center of your sermons on the wisdom literature, and emphasize the fear of the Lord as the place where wisdom can be found. Block defines *the fear of the Lord* as a "trusting awe" that results in obedience.[70] The fear of the Lord is what makes biblical wisdom stand out from other sources of wisdom in the world.[71] Unlike worldly sources, wisdom books are not meant to be resources for self-help; rather, they highlight the need for humans to fear and revere God.

Maclaren understood this quality of the wisdom, and he tied his applications to Christ by connecting the fear of the Lord in the Old Testament to a New Testament faith in Christ. Therefore, Maclaren's sermons can help preachers navigate the unique Christological challenges found in each wisdom book. As an example, scholars note that, while Christ is clearly presented in some portions of the book of Proverbs as the wisdom of God, individual proverbs within the book of Proverbs are not clearly Christocentric.[72] As discussed above, Maclaren modeled how to preach Christ from Proverbs while also doing justice to the authorial intent of the text. Preachers and teachers today can do the same. Point out biblical links between the person of Jesus Christ and the wisdom of God. Jesus' words and actions demonstrate how he is the image of the perfectly wise human and perfectly wise king. Furthermore, because Jesus fulfilled the requirements of biblical wisdom, he provides the grace when we fail to follow God. Maclaren's applications focused on God as the source of wisdom and the fear of God as the means of finding wisdom. He thus modeled how to wed these principles to applications when preaching the wisdom literature.

2. Use Illustrations and Address Young People.

Maclaren frequently told illustrations and stories to explain his text and help his hearers understand how it applied to them. Like Maclaren, use illustrations and stories to apply the theological doctrine grounded in the wisdom text. Wisdom describes reoccurring patterns of human experience. So, apply wisdom by narrating a scenario where the wisdom text can be

---

70. Block, "That They May All Fear Me," 72–73.

71. Arthurs, *Preaching with Variety*, 135.

72. E.g. Kaiser Jr., *Preaching and Teaching from the Old Testament*, 85; Block, "That They May All Fear Me," 68.

provoked. Search for events in your own past that demonstrate the truthfulness of the text. These stories help the audience picture how biblical wisdom applies in their own setting.

Maclaren was not only fond of illustrations when preaching the wisdom literature; he also used these texts as an opportunity to appeal to young people. While wisdom books apply to everyone because foolishness is not limited to a specific age, biblical wisdom has as its main audience the young.[73] The reason for this emphasis is that the young often are more likely to reject biblical wisdom for worldly foolishness. Maclaren was worried young people might be drawn away from the church by temptation and saw preaching to young people as an important part of his pulpit ministry. Likewise, consider directly addressing young people when preaching from the wisdom literature. These books prove an awesome opportunity for preachers today to appeal to younger generations. Doing so makes your applications consistent with the overall purpose of biblical wisdom.

3. Apply Wisdom in Relation to the Whole Canon.

Especially when in Ecclesiastes and Job, preachers and teachers must be sensitive to the entire revelation of Scripture. Some preachers may not share Maclaren's view on the overall structure and interpretation of Ecclesiastes and Job; however, they can still glean lessons from his sermons. Cross-references, especially those in relation to New Testament believers, can be very helpful in order to understand and apply Ecclesiastes. Maclaren understood that the New Testament provides further doctrinal words that complete or fill-out the doctrine expressed in Ecclesiastes; likewise, consider the New Testament when applying difficult passages.

Similarly, when approaching the book of Job, you may be tempted to bypass the speeches from Job's friends by preaching the whole book in one sermon, by focusing on the beginning and end narratives only, or by creating a topical series on reoccurring themes. Maclaren, on the other hand, demonstrated how to apply the individual chapters within the book of Job, including those containing the speeches from Job's friends. Like Maclaren, apply the book of Job by keeping your passage within its literary context. Understand that the friends did not approach the situation from a biblical perspective, so their words should not be read as entirely correct. Their

---

73. Smith, *Recapturing the Voice of God*, 150.

understanding of sorrow was too rigid and incomplete, and thus it was false.[74] Maclaren preached these texts with this characteristic in mind. Instead of shying away from the speeches made by Job's friends, explain how modern people still ask the same questions about suffering. Discuss how the friends' words both compare and contrast to the rest of Scripture, especially to the New Testament. Prove how the friends' wisdom was flawed, and then illuminate Christ as the ultimate answer to suffering.

Preachers can look to Maclaren as a model for how to apply the wisdom literature. Not all may agree with him on the structure and overall interpretation of the various wisdom books, but these issues should not prevent you from looking at his methods for application. Specifically, he exegeted the text within its historical and literary context. From this exegesis, he discovered the theological principle that was true of both the original audience and his hearers, and he lifted up the true source of wisdom as the fear and faith in Christ. These theological principles allowed him to apply the wisdom practically to his contemporary audience, even if the specific details in the text itself differed dramatically from the lives of Christians in his church.

SERMON BREAKDOWN: "TWO FORTRESSES"

Choosing one sermon to represent Maclaren's preaching from the wisdom literature is a difficult task because his approach varied depending on the book in which his text was found. However, his sermon "Two Fortresses" from Prov 28:1–11 provides one of the best overall examples of his preaching from the wisdom literature for two reasons. First, the text came from one of the largest and most difficult sub-genres of biblical wisdom literature, the proverbial sayings. Second, this sermon displays many of the characteristics that are common for all his sermons on the wisdom literature, including those from Job and Ecclesiastes. For these reasons, "Two Fortresses" gives readers a fairly comprehensive sample of his preaching from biblical wisdom.

As is typical of his sermons, Maclaren began by jumping straight into an explanation of his text. He told his audience that the proverbial sayings in Proverbs normally share little connection to their immediate context, but these verses were an exception since they were meant to show

---

74. Doriani, *Getting the Message*, 234; cf. Goldsworthy, *Preaching the Whole Bible as Christian Scripture*, 195.

a contrast. In the Hebrew the "contrast is even more emphatic" because the word translated "safe" was literally "set on high."[75] One verse depicted the man who is "lifted up above danger," while the other was of a man in "imaginary safety."[76] His main divisions set up a contrast between the two different fortresses, two different ways to get to the two refuges, and the two different consequences one faces depending on which refuge is sought.

He announced his first main point by declaring, "Consider then, first, the two fortresses."[77] One fortress has "the name of the Lord" while the other was "the rich man's wealth." The verses are placed side-by-side for "bitter emphasis." He defined the term "the name of the Lord" as "the Biblical expression for the whole character of God, as he has made it known to us or in other words, for God himself, as he has been pleased to reveal himself to mankind."[78] The term pointed to God as being self-existent and eternal and showed the character and heart of God. Ultimately Christ is the "revealer to our hearts of the heart of God."[79] Then, he gave the theological lesson from this portion of the text:

> The name that is 'the strong tower' is the name 'My Father!' a [sic] Father of infinite tenderness and wisdom and power. Oh! where [sic] can the child rest more quietly than on the mother's breast, where can the child be safer than in the circle of the father's arms?[80]

He turned to the second verse and the second fortress, which is built upon "the rich man's wealth." He explained that men, acting like "some poor lunatic," have always used "outward things" in order to try to feel secure and defended.[81] Maclaren took his audience to the story of the rich young ruler and reasoned Jesus understood that riches produce spiritual difficulties.[82]

He applied the text by universalizing the principle for his entire audience: "The illusion is one that besets us all. We are all tempted to make a defense of the things that we can see and handle."[83] A series of rhetorical

---

75. Maclaren, *Esther, Job, Proverbs and Ecclesiastes*, 210–11.
76. Maclaren, *Esther, Job, Proverbs and Ecclesiastes*, 211.
77. Maclaren, *Esther, Job, Proverbs and Ecclesiastes*, 211.
78. Maclaren, *Esther, Job, Proverbs and Ecclesiastes*, 211.
79. Maclaren, *Esther, Job, Proverbs and Ecclesiastes*, 212.
80. Maclaren, *Esther, Job, Proverbs and Ecclesiastes*, 213.
81. Maclaren, *Esther, Job, Proverbs and Ecclesiastes*, 213.
82. Maclaren, *Esther, Job, Proverbs and Ecclesiastes*, 213–14. The story of the rich young ruler can be found in Matt 19:16–30, Mark 10:17–31, and Luke 18:18–30.
83. Maclaren, *Esther, Job, Proverbs and Ecclesiastes*, 214.

questions followed and facilitated the application. He beseeched, "How many men are there in this chapel" and "how many of you" to demonstrate that his hearers too needed to heed the warning of the text. In fact, the danger of riches affect both the rich and poor alike. He urged them to see that physical riches will fade but spiritual riches are eternal; therefore, "turn it clean round, and you get the truth.... The real is the unseen beyond."[84] His first main point ended with an application crafted especially for young people. He exhorted them to lay the wisdom upon their hearts while they were young, warning that it is a delusion to believe possessions can be their "shield and stay."[85]

Maclaren moved to his second main point by voicing, "Consider next how to get into the true refuge."[86] He explained what the writer meant by "runneth into the name of the Lord" by illustrating a person straining to enter a stronghold before a disaster struck. The same picture of running and trusting in a fortress is used in the New Testament for putting one's faith in Jesus Christ: "Such a faith—the trust of mind, heart, and will—laying hold of the name of the Lord, makes us 'righteous.'"[87] Faith was how a person runs into the fortress of Christ, prepares the person to enter the fortress, and makes them "partakers of Christ's purity."[88]

He concluded this second main point with an application to seek Christ. He addressed his audience directly: "So my earnest question to you all is—Have you 'fled for refuge to lay hold' on that Saviour in whom God has set His name?"[89] A series of rhetorical questions challenged his listeners to test themselves and see if they had made Christ their refuge by faith. Finally, there is the comfort that, if they sought Christ, "there shall no evil befall you."[90]

Maclaren announced his final main point with the words, "So we have, lastly, what comes of sheltering in these two refuges."[91] He reminded his audience that the phrase "is safe" was "accurately as well as picturesquely

---

84. Maclaren, *Esther, Job, Proverbs and Ecclesiastes*, 214.
85. Maclaren, *Esther, Job, Proverbs and Ecclesiastes*, 215–16.
86. Maclaren, *Esther, Job, Proverbs and Ecclesiastes*, 216.
87. Maclaren, *Esther, Job, Proverbs and Ecclesiastes*, 217.
88. Maclaren, *Esther, Job, Proverbs and Ecclesiastes*, 218.
89. Maclaren, *Esther, Job, Proverbs and Ecclesiastes*, 218.
90. Maclaren, *Esther, Job, Proverbs and Ecclesiastes*, 218.
91. Maclaren, *Esther, Job, Proverbs and Ecclesiastes*, 218.

rendered by 'is set aloft.'"[92] He pictured a fugitive taken up into a firm battlement far from his pursuers and their attacks. Then, that firm battlement was contrasted with the weaker battlement wealth afforded. He exclaimed, "They can keep the rifle-bullets from us," but when "the big siege guns get into position and begin to play," then the defenses from material wealth crash down "like the pasteboard helmet which looked as good as if it had been steel, and did admirably as long as no sword struck it."[93]

Maclaren flowed into his final application—his audience should put their faith in Christ. He argued, "There is only one thing that will keep us peaceful and unharmed, and that is to trust our poor shelterless lives and sinful souls to the Saviour who has died for us."[94] Using the language of warfare found in the proverb, he compared the benefits of following Christ as if one is fleeing behind a defensive wall.[95] His sermon closed with an evangelistic appeal: "I beseech you, make no delay. Escape! flee [*sic*] for your life! A growing host of evil marches swift against you. Take Christ for your defence and cry to him."[96]

DISCUSSION QUESTIONS

1. What makes biblical wisdom stand out from other genres such as the law? Why should we heed biblical wisdom?

2. According to the Bible, what is the key attitude one must have in order to understand and appreciate the wisdom of God?

3. Try finding text-grounded applications for Prov 26:1–12, Job 8, and Eccl 1:1–11.

---

92. Maclaren, *Esther, Job, Proverbs and Ecclesiastes*, 218.
93. Maclaren, *Esther, Job, Proverbs and Ecclesiastes*, 219.
94. Maclaren, *Esther, Job, Proverbs and Ecclesiastes*, 219–20.
95. Maclaren, *Esther, Job, Proverbs and Ecclesiastes*, 220.
96. Maclaren, *Esther, Job, Proverbs and Ecclesiastes*, 220.

6

Proclaiming the Word
Prophecy and Epistles

"Christians are the stones, apostles and prophets the builders, and Christ Himself the chief corner-stone."

—Alexander Maclaren

The prophetic and epistolary literature actually share much in common. Both were written by divinely inspired men who were expositing the practical implications of God's previous revelation. Furthermore, they wrote in an expositional style using arguments and focusing on logic, which flows quite naturally into sermonic forms. All of these qualities make the epistles and prophets not only similar to one another but also considered by many to be easier to preach and teach.

Nevertheless, reading the epistles and prophets is not all sunshine. Both forms of communication were heavily reliant on Old Testament stories, customs, and laws, some of which modern audiences may not know well. Their words were addressed to specific audiences in specific locations, facing specific temptations. In essence, they function similar to a phone conversation, but the reader is only hearing one side of the phone call. For these reasons, the issues and commands in these books sometimes sound odd to contemporary listeners. This disparity is more readily obvious in the prophets, but it can even plague the pastor when in the epistles.

While we often feel at home in the epistles due to their New Testament nature, the prophetic books tend to be viewed with trepidation. This chapter, therefore, will focus more on Maclaren's sermons from the prophetic literature. Maclaren was lauded in his day for preaching the Old Testament, and the prophetic material was no exception. One reviewer said of his two-volume work on Isaiah that he expected it to be a "most popular publication on the great Hebrew prophet" for preachers in his day.[1] Maclaren studied the text to discover the theological message the prophet or epistle conveys and then applied this theological message to the people of his day. He can serve as a model for how to preach the prophets and epistles.

HOW TO MODEL MACLAREN IN THE PROPHETS AND EPISTLES

In a sermon on Eph 2:20, Maclaren spoke about the connection between the prophets and epistles: "Here [in Eph 2:20] Jesus is designated as the foundation stone which . . . binds [the prophets and apostles] strongly together, it is more natural to see in the prophets the representatives of the great teachers of the old dispensation as the apostles were of the new."[2] For this reason, Maclaren's sermons in the epistles were very similar to his sermons in the Old Testament prophets, and much of what he did when applying the prophets was repeated when applying the New Testament epistles as well.

Maclaren saw the prophets as both foretelling the future and applying the Torah to the context of their day. Though foretelling is not so prevalent in the epistles, apocalyptic elements are found throughout these New Testament books. When the epistles contain apocalyptic elements, they imitate the foretelling mandate found in the prophets. In regards to predicting future events, the prophets could accurately see the future.[3] The visions were not allegorical depictions of present realities, but rather they accurately described eschatological history or the life of Christ.[4] The prophets were not giving predictions based on natural observations, like how a meteorologist may predict the weather; rather, they were revealing a message from God regarding what lies ahead. Maclaren commented in one sermon about the prophetic office,

1. Anonymous, "Work and Workers," 393.
2. Maclaren, *Ephesians*, 119.
3. Maclaren, *Conquering Christ*, 117; Maclaren, *Isaiah: Chaps. I to XLVIII*, 57.
4. Maclaren, *Ezekiel, Daniel, and the Minor Prophets*, 344.

We mutilate the grand idea of the prophet in Israel if we think of his work as mainly prediction, and we mutilate it no less if we exclude prediction from it. We mutilate it still more fatally if we try to account for it on naturalistic principles, and fail to see in the prophet a man directly conscious of a divine call, or to hear in his words the solemn accents of the voice of God.[5]

Maclaren believed, however, the prophets could be unaware of how their prophecies would be ultimately fulfilled.[6] Maclaren argued that prophecies frequently describe multiple future events with wide gaps between them, but the prophets themselves visualized the events as occuring together.[7] Moreover, Maclaren believed the prophets saw the Messiah but only "dimly."[8] They could even prophesy about Christ without realizing it.[9] The prophets' original audience likewise could be unaware of how each prophecy ultimately finds its fulfillment in Jesus.[10] The reason Scripture can be fulfilled in Christ, according to Maclaren, without the prophets' or original audiences' express knowledge is because the Holy Spirit is the ultimate author of the prophecies.[11]

While foretelling was one task, the authors primarily addressed issues in their present society. Some recent scholars have called this task "forthtelling."[12] They directed their messages toward those who had the form of godliness but did not practice it in their daily lives, and as a result, their messages often had polarizing effects.[13] It repelled many from God, but for a few it roused them to follow God.[14] The epistle writers are doing the same for the church related to the crucifixion, person, and works of Jesus Christ. Consequently, Maclaren produced a similar preaching method in both the prophets and the epistles. Preachers who wish to mirror Maclaren's preaching from these genres should consider the following steps.

5. Maclaren, *Deuteronomy, Joshua, Judges, Ruth, and First Book of Samuel*, 20.

6. Maclaren, *Isaiah: Chaps. I to XLVIII*, 48, 61; Maclaren, *Deuteronomy, Joshua, Judges, Ruth, and First Book of Samuel*, 223.

7. Maclaren, *Ezekiel, Daniel, and the Minor Prophets*, 346–47.

8. Maclaren, *Isaiah: Chaps. I to XLVIII*, 53.

9. Maclaren, *Rosary of Christian Graces*, 160.

10. Maclaren, *Isaiah: Chaps. I to XLVIII*, 51.

11. Maclaren, *Isaiah: Chaps. I to XLVIII*, 49.

12. See Doriani, *Getting the Message*, 232; Osborne, *Hermeneutical Spiral*, 265; Kaiser Jr., *Preaching and Teaching from the Old Testament*, 111.

13. Maclaren, *Ezekiel, Daniel, and the Minor Prophets*, 337–38.

14. Maclaren, *Isaiah: Chaps. I to XLVIII*, 22.

1. Understand the Content of the Prophecy or Epistle.

Maclaren almost always began with a description of what the text meant to the original readers. His explanations, therefore, were heavily reliant on the historical context.[15] In the same vein, teachers today need to explain historical concepts that might be unknown to contemporary audiences and show why these concepts are important for understanding the text.[16] Even when focusing on an image or theme within the text, reveal how your interpretation is within the bounds of the historical context.[17]

In like manner, keep your sermons within the boundaries of the literary context. Maclaren often showed how his passage related to the surrounding paragraphs and even the books as a whole.[18] Similarly, look at the message of the whole book when interpreting the passage. For example, in one sermon Maclaren acknowledged that a key theme of the book of Hosea is the need for repentance, and he believed that this overall theme should be considered when studying each individual text.[19] He thus treated the immediate and canonical context of his text as vital for understanding the biblical passage.

After revealing the historical and literary context, explain the content of the text itself. Point out significant aspects of the original languages that are missed in English translations.[20] Explain any figures of speech in the text that might not be understood.[21] Analogies may also be a useful tool to help people grasp the text and connect it their own lives.[22] In addition, if the prophetic or epistolary has narrative qualities, then vividly retell the story, similar to the historic books and Gospels.[23] Maclaren was a master

---

15. Maclaren, *Ezekiel, Daniel, and the Minor Prophets*, 108, 115; Maclaren, *Isaiah: Chaps. I to XLVIII*, 18, 43, 48.

16. Maclaren, *Ezekiel, Daniel, and the Minor Prophets*, 94–99, 100; Maclaren, *Conquering Christ*, 112.

17. Maclaren, *Ezekiel, Daniel, and the Minor Prophets*, 177–84, 328–37.

18. Maclaren, *Isaiah: Chaps. I to XLVIII*, 57; Maclaren, *Ezekiel, Daniel, and the Minor Prophets*, 76, 101.

19. Maclaren, *Ezekiel, Daniel, and the Minor Prophets*, 135.

20. Maclaren, *Isaiah: Chaps. I to XLVIII*, 50, 59, 60; Maclaren, *Ezekiel, Daniel, and the Minor Prophets*, 122, 139, 187, 190.

21. E.g. Maclaren, *Ezekiel, Daniel, and the Minor Prophets*, 131–32, where he discussed what Hosea might have been referring to when he mentions the dew, the lily, and the olive.

22. E.g. see his analogy between sin and snakes in Maclaren, *Ezekiel, Daniel, and the Minor Prophets*, 112.

23. Maclaren, *Ezekiel, Daniel, and the Minor Prophets*, 48–54, 76–83, 189–96;

at explaining epistolary and prophetic passages using such vivid, figurative language, which contributed to his preaching power.

2. Find the Author's Theological Lesson in the Prophecy or Epistle.

After Maclaren explained the text, he revealed the theological lesson the author purposed to convey. These authors intended not merely to teach historic facts but to proclaim theological truth. Maclaren commented, "But while thus there is a plain piece of political history in the words, they are also the statements of general principles which apply to every individual soul and its relation to the kingdom, the gentle kingdom, of our Lord and Saviour Jesus Christ."[24]

Maclaren's transitions from exegesis to theological significance occurred so smoothly that they are easy to miss. He spoke as if the prophets and epistles were directly addressed to his audience. Preachers today can use processes similar to Maclaren. For example, in many ways, God continues to act today like he did in the time of the biblical writers.[25] Therefore, promises God made through the prophets to Israel are still applicable to Christian audiences; though, they may apply to the eschaton period and not contemporary earthly life.[26] Humans also continue to react to God's divine activity in the same way as the ancient Israel and the early church did.[27] Most importantly, the sins the writers are addressing still plague modern hearers.[28]

Maclaren's sermons from the prophets contained one noticeable difference when compared to his sermons on other portions of Scripture. He treated prophets as if they intentionally used objects, people, and illustrative images to symbolize theological truths.[29] Even visions can be both accurate

---

Maclaren, *Isaiah: Chaps. I to XLVIII*, 18–23.

24. Maclaren, *Isaiah: Chaps. I to XLVIII*, 46.

25. Maclaren, *Ezekiel, Daniel, and the Minor Prophets*, 355; Maclaren, *Isaiah: Chaps. I to XLVIII*, 18, 22, 28.

26. Maclaren, *Conquering Christ*, 45.

27. Maclaren, *Isaiah: Chaps. I to XLVIII*, 21; Maclaren, *Ezekiel, Daniel, and the Minor Prophets*, 340–41, 355.

28. Maclaren, *Ezekiel, Daniel, and the Minor Prophets*, 108, 120–21.

29. Maclaren, *Conquering Christ*, 113; Maclaren, *Isaiah: Chaps. I to XLVIII*, 34; Maclaren, *Rosary of Christian Graces*, 162.

prophecies of future events and metaphors describing theological truths.[30] Thus, he discovered the theological lesson by focusing on the details of the text and connecting them to the universal nature of God and human sin.

3. Look for How the Prophets and Epistles Point to Jesus.

Because the prophets and epistles frequently spoke against sin, Maclaren did not hesitate to draw his audiences to Christ as the solution to the sin problem in the text. He believed the purpose of Scripture was to reveal who God is, and Jesus is the fullest revelation of God's work and character in Scripture. He maintained that the life of Christ sheds light on the Bible and is essential to applying it correctly.[31] Furthermore, the hope of the Messiah was the link between the prophets and the New Testament epistles.[32]

In this way, Maclaren treated the prophets more as heralds of the messianic king than as foretellers of the immediate future. If the text was not explicitly messianic, he explained what the passage meant to the original readers before making a connection to Christ.[33] At the very least, Maclaren described Christ as a second, "deeper significance" of the text.[34] In this way Jesus would be a major portion of the sermon regardless of the topic addressed by the text.

Maclaren modeled several means for preachers for how to preach Christ. For instance, point out the times when Christ clearly fulfilled a prophecy.[35] References to the Davidic monarchy can be connected to the Messiah and his kingdom.[36] Jesus also is the ultimate example of the doctrine or action proclaimed in the text.[37] An image or metaphor in the text can find its true fulfillment in Christ as well.[38] If you are describing an activity of God, then reveal how that activity is fulfilled in the person or works of the Son of God.[39] For prophetic literature in particular, how the original

---

30. Maclaren, *Conquering Christ*, 117–18.
31. Pace, "Alexander Maclaren," 80, 85.
32. Sellers, "Other Times, Other Ministries," 190.
33. E.g. Maclaren, *Ezekiel, Daniel, and the Minor Prophets*, 183–84.
34. Maclaren, *Rosary of Christian Graces*, 160–61.
35. Maclaren, *Isaiah: Chaps. I to XLVIII*, 59.
36. For example, Maclaren, *Isaiah: Chaps. I to XLVIII*, 51.
37. Maclaren, *Rosary of Christian Graces*, 165–66.
38. Maclaren, *Rosary of Christian Graces*, 167.
39. Maclaren, *Isaiah and Jeremiah*, 274; Maclaren, *Rosary of Christian Graces*, 166–67.

Israelites related to God may be compared to how Christians now relate to Christ.[40] Even the very words the authors spoke can be compared to Christ's words in the Gospels.[41]

Maclaren's most frequent means of preaching Christ was to show how repentance and faith in Christ is the solution to the sin described in the text. For example, in his sermon on Hos 13:9, Maclaren masterfully moved from Hosea to the gospel by saying,

> Our text has wrapped up in it the broad gospel that all our self-inflicted destruction may be arrested, and all the evil which brought it about swept away. God is ready to prove Himself our true and only Helper.... All our guilt is ours; all the help is His; His work is to conquer and cast out our sins, to heal our sicknesses, to soothe our sorrows. And he has Himself vindicated His great name of our help when He has revealed Himself as 'the God and Father of our Lord and Saviour Jesus Christ.'[42]

Thus Maclaren's preaching was thoroughly Christocentric when in the epistles and prophets.

4. Apply the Theological Lesson of the Prophecy or Epistle.

After Maclaren explained the text and its theological principle, he applied the passage to his audience. Similar to Maclaren, preachers today can use multiple stylistic changes to signal that you are moving to applications. For one, address people directly with second-person pronouns or with imperative sentences.[43] The phrase "let us" can be employed strategically to exhort the audience to apply the text to themselves.[44] A speaker tag or interjection may grab people's attention and jolt them into hearing what the Scripture says.[45] Point out obligations that your hearers ought to do if the

---

40. Maclaren, *Isaiah and Jeremiah*, 289, 292; Maclaren, *Ezekiel, Daniel, and the Minor Prophets*, 357.

41. Maclaren, *Isaiah: Chaps. I to XLVIII*, 61; Maclaren, *Ezekiel, Daniel, and the Minor Prophets*, 122–23, 337, 346.

42. Maclaren, *Ezekiel, Daniel, and the Minor Prophets*, 113.

43. Maclaren, *Conquering Christ*, 120; Maclaren, *Rosary of Christian Graces*, 164; Maclaren, *Ezekiel, Daniel, and the Minor Prophets*, 354.

44. Maclaren, *Isaiah: Chaps. I to XLVIII*, 26, 28; Maclaren, *Conquering Christ*, 120; Maclaren, *Rosary of Christian Graces*, 166.

45. Maclaren, *Isaiah: Chaps. I to XLVIII*, 28, 32–33, 35; Maclaren, *Isaiah and Jeremiah*, 277, 286, 289, 293.

text's doctrine is true.⁴⁶ Turn the theological propositions into conditional sentences and argue for what people should do to receive or avoid the results described in the text.⁴⁷ On occasion, challenge them with rhetorical questions, asking them if they are following the writer's message.⁴⁸ These stylistic changes help flag applications for your hearers.

Maclaren believed the biblical text only had one meaning. To give an example, he once insisted, "The words of my text have often, and terribly, been misunderstood. And I wish now to try to bring out their true meaning and bearing. They have a message for us quite as much as they had for the people who originally received them."⁴⁹ Furthermore, the practical instructions the writers were giving were never random but always grounded on the unchanging theological principles in the text.⁵⁰ While the meaning and theological principle of the passage remains unchanged, application of the principle could change slightly from audience to audience.⁵¹ Most preachers see this relevance of the epistles; Maclaren, however, also treated the prophets as immediately applicable to Christians because they spoke to human experiences common throughout time and culture:

> A true prophet's words are of universal application, even when they are most specially addressed to a particular audience. Just because this indictment was so true of Judah, is it true of all men, for it is not concerned with details peculiar to a long-past period and state of society, but with the broad generalities common to us all.⁵²

He claimed preachers have theological warrant to apply the prophets' and epistles' messages to their own audiences. As Pace rightly argues, "Maclaren recognized the immediate relevance of prophetic texts."⁵³

---

46. Maclaren, *Isaiah and Jeremiah*, 273, 288, 291; Maclaren, *Rosary of Christian Graces*, 169; Maclaren, *Ezekiel, Daniel, and the Minor Prophets*, 334, 341, 353.

47. Maclaren, *Isaiah and Jeremiah*, 274, 293; Maclaren, *Conquering Christ*, 117; Maclaren, *Rosary of Christian Graces*, 164, 169; Maclaren, *Ezekiel, Daniel, and the Minor Prophets*, 346, 357.

48. Maclaren, *Isaiah and Jeremiah*, 286; Maclaren, *Ezekiel, Daniel, and the Minor Prophets*, 7, 335, 357.

49. Maclaren, *Ezekiel, Daniel, and the Minor Prophets*, 100.

50. Maclaren, *Isaiah and Jeremiah*, 283, 284.

51. Maclaren, *Ezekiel, Daniel, and the Minor Prophets*, 29.

52. Maclaren, *Isaiah: Chaps. I to XLVIII*, 1–2.

53. Pace, "Alexander Maclaren," 79.

This is not to say that application may come easily, and Maclaren modeled what to do when a text does not seem immediately applicable. He first revealed the application the author intended for the original audience. Then, he transitioned to the contemporary application by focusing on the universal theology of the text. In one sermon Maclaren described the text's meaning to the original audience, and then he said, "But we may dismiss the immediate application of the words for the sake of looking at the general principle which underlies them."[54] Lastly, he gave examples of how the text applies to people today.

Maclaren had several theological principles he used to bridge from exegesis to application which preachers and teachers today should consider. First, God's character remains the same throughout time, and God continues to act in ways similar, though perhaps not exact, to what he did in ancient days.[55] This means believers back then acted on faith in the same God as Christians do today.[56] Furthermore, if the text describes a consequence of being near God, this result in some way holds true for audiences today as well.[57] For this same reason, you can urge your audiences to emulate the prophets and apostles, who serve as examples of how to have a right relationship with God.[58]

Not only does God's nature not change, but basic human nature does not change regardless of time and space: Maclaren said, "Human nature was very much the same in the exiles that listened to Ezekiel on the banks of the Chebar and in Manchester to-day [sic]."[59] For example, humans react to God the same way today as they did in the past.[60] Preachers thus can focus on people's propensity today to commit the same sins which are described in the text. Maclaren argued, "Change the name, and the tale is told of us."[61] This was Maclaren's most frequent means of applying these texts. He urged his audiences to avoid the same sin the original audience faced or avoid

---

54. Maclaren, *Isaiah and Jeremiah*, 258; cf. Maclaren, *Isaiah: Chaps. I to XLVIII*, 45.

55. E.g. Maclaren, *Ezekiel, Daniel, and the Minor Prophets*, 82, 168.

56. Maclaren, *Isaiah and Jeremiah*, 292.

57. Maclaren, *Ezekiel, Daniel, and the Minor Prophets*, 137; Maclaren, *Conquering Christ*, 119–20.

58. Maclaren, *Isaiah: Chaps. I to XLVIII*, 29; Maclaren, *Isaiah and Jeremiah*, 289, 291, 293.

59. Maclaren, *Ezekiel, Daniel, and the Minor Prophets*, 10.

60. Maclaren, *Ezekiel, Daniel, and the Minor Prophets*, 82.

61. Maclaren, *Isaiah: Chaps. I to XLVIII*, 17.

similar circumstances today that cause the same sin.[62] If a sin is culturally or historically bound, Maclaren focused on the theological principle and then found a similar application today to the situation of the original audience.[63] Therefore, Maclaren used the theological truth in the text as a way to find analogous situations in his day to which the text might apply.

If you are in a prophetic book, read New Testament passages that speak to the same topic to show how the problem the prophets faced remains relevant in New Testament times.[64] If a prophetic text is not directly applicable because it includes Old Covenant stipulations, then consider interpreting the texts eschatologically or soteriologically. Some passages that were true of ancient Israel in this life are true for Christians in the eschaton.[65] Also, the physical consequences of sin and repentance under the old covenant can be metaphors for spiritual realities under the new covenant.[66] In this way, the prophets are still applicable for Christians even though they were tied to the old covenant.

Since such preaching focuses on sinful similarities between the original audience and today's audience, the most important application you can make from the prophets and epistles is to call people to turn to Christ for grace and hope. In fact, Maclaren's greatest strength when preaching from the prophets and epistles was in his willingness to declare the hope of redemption through repentance. You can preach the gospel powerfully even from passages where the hope of grace is not explicitly stated if you understand how each text is related to redemptive history. By way of an example, in one sermon, Maclaren told his audience, even though the text before them contained the certainty of judgment, "Do not believe that there are any bounds or end to God's forbearing pleading with men in this life."[67] Maclaren pointed out how prophecies were framed by the hope of redemption that are proclaimed at the end of the book.[68] The very fact that the judgment passage exists proves God is "wooing" people back to

---

62. Maclaren, *Isaiah and Jeremiah*, 289; Maclaren, *Isaiah: Chaps. I to XLVIII*, 13–17.

63. Maclaren, *Isaiah and Jeremiah*, 272; Maclaren, *Ezekiel, Daniel, and the Minor Prophets*, 329.

64. Maclaren, *Isaiah: Chaps. I to XLVIII*, 32; Maclaren, *Ezekiel, Daniel, and the Minor Prophets*, 335.

65. Maclaren, *Isaiah and Jeremiah*, 260–61.

66. Maclaren, *Isaiah: Chaps. I to XLVIII*, 9; Maclaren, *Isaiah and Jeremiah*, 282–83.

67. Maclaren, *Ezekiel, Daniel, and the Minor Prophets*, 101.

68. Maclaren, *Ezekiel, Daniel, and the Minor Prophets*, 102, 113.

him.[69] You also can point out how the pronouncements of judgment in the books are balanced by the hopeful oracles of God's grace. The commands and warnings in prophets and epistles always contain a degree of hope and forgiveness even if that hope is only implied.[70]

Furthermore, God's grace through faith in Jesus is needed not only for salvation but also ongoing sanctification. Maclaren stated, "We are most firmly bound to God, not by our resolves, but by our experience of His all-sufficient mercy. Fill the heart with that wine of the kingdom, and bitter or poisonous draughts will find no entrance into the cup."[71] Therefore, applications from the prophets and epistles should go beyond mere obedience to God and the cessation of sin. Urge people to seek Christ as the answer to their sinfulness. Do not be content with preaching judgment or commands alone, but rather connect judgment and commands to the redemption in Jesus Christ. In this way Maclaren kept his applications grounded on authorial intent.

MAIN TAKEAWAYS FROM MACLAREN FOR THE PROPHETS AND EPISTLES

Pace identifies Maclaren's method of application from the prophets as his lasting contribution to expository preaching, stating, "The beautiful blend of textual exposition and contemporary relevance is perhaps the most significant contribution Maclaren made to the field of preaching."[72] Expositors can still glean lessons on how to apply the Old Testament prophets and New Testament epistles from reading his sermons. Three practices in particular are vital for preachers and teachers to study and consider when in an epistle or prophetic book.

1. Don't Skip Literary and Historical Exegesis.

The context is important when interpreting and applying the prophetic and epistolary literature. Even in sermons where Maclaren's main points focused on theology and application, he began his sermon with an overview

---

69. Maclaren, *Ezekiel, Daniel, and the Minor Prophets*, 101.
70. Maclaren, *Ezekiel, Daniel, and the Minor Prophets*, 195.
71. Maclaren, *Ezekiel, Daniel, and the Minor Prophets*, 130.
72. Pace, "Alexander Maclaren," 85.

of the historical situation. Only after studying its historical context did he move to potential applications. The prophets essentially were expositing Old Testament Scripture and conveyed relevant and practical applications for their audience. The epistolary authors in similar fashion were preachers who exposited the theological and practical implications of Christ's incarnation, crucifixion, resurrection, and return. Their messages are historically bound; thus it is imperative that you read this literature within its historical context before applying it to modern circumstances. Both the larger historical background of the book and the specific context of each passage are important for correct application. One of the major mistakes preachers make is acting as if a prophetic utterance connects directly to a modern situation when the historical context demonstrates that it is at best only tangentially connected.[73] Furthermore, knowing the events and people described in the Bible can help bring to light the meaning of obscure texts. Thus, identifying the historical context is crucial for those who want to understand and apply the epistles and prophets to Christians in today's context. Maclaren achieved this emphasis in his preaching.

Moreover, the literary context is essential for properly preaching a prophetic or epistolary text. Not only the immediate context, but the message of the entire book must be considered because the literary context provides insight into the specific situation the authors were addressing and why they were writing. Since the majority of Maclaren's sermons focus on one or two verses, one might assume he did not consider the literary context. This assumption is untrue. Even when he focused on a single verse, he tended to explain the chapter in which it was found in the introduction of his sermon. His interpretation and applications were grounded in his understanding of the literary context. Maclaren's focus on the overall historical and literary context of the prophets illustrates for preachers how proper exegesis is vital for applying the prophets and epistles correctly.

2. Connect Applications to the Unchanging Nature of God and Sin.

In addition to proper exegesis, Maclaren also demonstrated for pastors how the theological content of the text can provide a bridge between the original audience and accurate applications for today. After exegeting the text, he focused on what the text taught about God and God's relationship with humanity. For Maclaren, these lessons have not changed over time because

---

73. Köstenberger and Patterson, *Biblical Interpretation*, 771–72.

God has not changed; therefore, what the authors said about who God is and what he does can serve as a bridge from the text to today.

Not only has God not changed since the biblical era, but humanity's tendency to sin also has remained consistent. The sins the authors dealt with are still seen in contemporary society, and they still need condemning by preachers. For this reason, the text's focus on sin can be a bridge from the original audiences to audiences today. The writers' exhortations and rebukes should still be heard in churches today. Specifically, they reveal to Christians how correct belief should lead to correct action. Look, therefore, for situations in your own context that are analogous to the sinful conditions the authors were addressing and apply the theology of the text to your situation.

While the sinful nature of the original audience is shared with Christians, one mistake you must avoid when preaching the prophetic works is directly applying the stipulations of the old covenant to the church. Instead, consider how the prophetic message relates to those under the new covenant rather than the old. For example, no political nation today stands in the same relationship to God as Israel, and some of the blessings and curses of the old covenant may be relegated to eternity for Christians. Maclaren demonstrated how to preach practical new covenant applications that also are appropriate to an old covenant text. He excelled at showing his audience how the sinful nature of the original audience continued to be reflected in his day.

3. Extend Hope through Repentance and Faith In Jesus.

The prophets and epistles extend the hope of God's grace to their readers. That hope comes through repentance, regardless of whether it is made explicit in the text itself. The judgment and commandment pericopes are often tempered by salvific pericopes in other places in the books, proving the authors never divorced forceful instruction from the hope of salvation. Nogalski states, "Repentance, not pride, in the face of calamity and threat offers the only hope. . . . Restoration begins when proper attention is paid to YHWH."[74] Therefore, present to your audience both the concept of sin and the hope of God's grace.

Maclaren offered this hope to his congregation as well. He frequently called his hearers to repentance, and his main method of providing hope from sin was to emphasize the person and works of Jesus Christ. His preaching was consistently Christocentric. In the same vein, trace the flow

---

74. Nogalski, "Recurring Themes in the Book of the Twelve," 136.

of redemptive history from the prophets to the New Testament epistles and ultimately to hope in Christ. Avoid jumping to allusions or allegories as a means of preaching Christ. Instead, link the command to repent in the prophets and epistles to the grace that God provides in Christ. Smith says it well: "Thus, the message the prophets speak is the same as we modern preachers speak. We tell people of the hope that is in Christ."[75] An emphasis on hope by repentance and redemption in Christ can prevent the preacher from making his sermon merely a rebuke of moral problems and societal injustices. A Christological application is what makes the sermon distinctly Christian. Maclaren frequently urged his hearers towards faith in Christ when preaching from the prophets and epistles, a practice that would flourish today.

The need to preach Christ correctly becomes more apparent when preaching the apocalyptic texts or visions of the future. Expositors sometimes fall into two errors when expositing these oracles. Some preachers go straight to Christ or the eschaton without reference to the original context. Others remain in the past without noting the text's relevance for today's Christians, but apocalyptic visions were not spoken in a vacuum. Both New and Old Testament authors wrote prophesies in order to evoke a response and to get their readers to do something; therefore, the original purpose for a vision or prophecy should be expounded first before showing how it relates to Christ or the end times. In this way, you can guard against linking a text to a modern situation to the neglect of authorial intent.

Maclaren demonstrated how to do this well. He applied prophecies and visions of the future only after discussing the theology the author was trying to teach. He used exegesis and theological interpretation as the grounds for his application, not speculations about the future. This method prevented him from moving too far from the author's intended purpose when applying the visions of the future in the epistles and prophets.

Maclaren can serve as a model for text-driven preachers on how to accurately apply the prophets and the epistles. He carefully exegeted the text based on the literary and historical context in which it was found and employed this exegesis to find the theological message the writer intended to convey. He believed God, sin, and hope through repentance had not changed despite the cultural and historical gap between the original audience and the people of his day. These theological truths became the hinge connecting the historic character of the text to relevant applications for his

---

75. Smith, *Recapturing the Voice of God*, 168, 172.

hearers. Finally, he showed how the text was fulfilled in the person and works of Christ. He consistently pointed his congregation to Christ as the answer to sin and the person in whom hope is found through repentance.

SERMON BREAKDOWN: "BLEMISHED OFFERINGS"

Maclaren's sermon "Blemished Offerings" from Mal 1:8 can provide a good example of his peaching for several reasons.[76] First, he took only one verse as his chosen text. While he preached full paragraphs on occasion, the majority of his sermons on the prophets and epistles focused on one or two verses. Second, this sermon exemplified his method of explaining the text in the introduction and then using theology to connect the text to applications in the body of the sermon.

Maclaren began the sermon with the literary and historical context of the text. He told his audience the verse is found in a section of Scripture where the prophet is rebuking the priests for exchanging quality animals for less costly ones. He noted that, within the historical culture of the day, the priests might have believed this exchange was an acceptable way of achieving economic gain. After this summary of the immediate context, he quickly explained the text with rhetorical flair:

> Will an offering of that sort be considered a compliment or an insult? Do you think it will smooth your way or help your suit with him? Surely God deserves as much reverts as the deputy of Artaxerxes. Surely what is not good enough for a Persian satrap is not good enough for the Lord of Hosts. Offer it to the governor, will he be pleased with it? Will he accept thy person?[77]

He then announced the theological thrust of the passage and how he planned to apply it to his congregation. He bridged the text to his hearers by focusing on the priests' sin. He claimed that Christians continue to struggle with the same sinful tendency of the priests: "Now, it seems to me that this cheap religion of the priests, and this scathing irony of the Prophet's counsel need little modification to fit us very closely."[78] With this theological bridge, he moved into the body of his sermon.

---

76. Maclaren, *Ezekiel, Daniel, and the Minor Prophets*, 328–37.
77. Maclaren, *Ezekiel, Daniel, and the Minor Prophets*, 328.
78. Maclaren, *Ezekiel, Daniel, and the Minor Prophets*, 329.

He announced his first main point by saying, "We note the startling and strange contrast which the text suggests."[79] He showed his audience how to move from the specific rebuke of the text to his church's context by generalizing the priests' actions. The sinful actions of the priests still rear their head in their congregation, though the specific actions may look slightly different:

> The diseased lamb was laid without scruple or hesitation on God's altar, and not one of these tricky priests durst have taken it to Court in order to secure favour there. Generalize that, and it comes to this—the gifts that we lavish on men are the condemnation of the gifts that we bring to God; and further, we should be ashamed to offer to men what we are not in the least ashamed to bring to God.[80]

Maclaren applied the text by giving three situations that "illustrate" how the same sinful problem raises its head in contemporary times. First, some regularly live with a greater love toward their families than toward God. Second, others demonstrate greater trust toward one another than toward God. Finally, many show greater submission and obedience to people than to God. He summarizes these three by contending, "And so I might go on, all round the horizon of our human nature, and signalize the difference that exists between the blemished sacrifices which each part of our being dares to bring to God and expects of him to accept, and the sacrifices, unblemished and spotless, which we carry one another."[81]

He told his audience he wanted to add one more application that more directly spoke to the specific subject Malachi was rebuking. The amount of financial support Christians put toward luxury far outweighs the amount of financial support they put toward Christian endeavors. Many of the hearers in Maclaren's congregation were proud that England had spent ten million pounds on war efforts that year; however, he pointed out the yearly contributions toward missionary efforts had not equaled a tenth of that amount. Maclaren took on the forthtelling spirit of the prophet as he closed this first main point:

> I do not suppose that there is one of us that applies the underlying principle of our text, of giving God our best, to this work. . . . The contrast between what we lavish on other things and what we give

---

79. Maclaren, *Ezekiel, Daniel, and the Minor Prophets*, 329.
80. Maclaren, *Ezekiel, Daniel, and the Minor Prophets*, 329.
81. Maclaren, *Ezekiel, Daniel, and the Minor Prophets*, 230–31.

for God's work in the world, is a shameful contrast, like that other which the Prophet gibbeted with his indignant eloquence.[82]

Maclaren then announced his second main point: "And now let me come to another point—viz., that we have here suggested and implied the true law and principle on which all Christian giving of all sorts is to be regulated. And that is—give the best."[83] He claimed the text implied a general principle: unblemished animals were the accepted gift for both God and government officials. Christians no longer offer animal sacrifices, but the theological principle was still applicable if it was made abstract (or "expanded").[84]

What followed was a series of steps that should result in Christians giving more generously. First, Christ giving himself up on the cross serves as the foundation for giving. Maclaren appealed to his audience to surrender their lives to Christ with a rhetorical question: "Do you believe that? Do you believe it about yourself? If you do, then the next step becomes certain. That gift, truly received by any man, will infallibly lead to a kindred (though infinitely more inferior) self-surrender."[85] He illustrated this application with two analogies. Christians should relate to Christ like how smaller celestial bodies orbit around a larger body or like how smaller states are accepted into the British Empire. Complete surrender to Christ is the first step to giving generously.

The second step is to view possessions differently—as a joyful stewardship. Christians ought to realize "capacities, faculties, means, opportunities, powers of brain and heart and mind, and everything else—they all belong to Him."[86] Christians should have the same mentality as medieval lords who knelt and handed the rights to their properties over to their kings. Likewise, he argued giving money to God should be an act of giving up ourselves. He exhorted,

> A great many of us put our sixpence, or our half-crown, or our sovereign, into the plate, and no part of ourselves goes with it, except a little twinge of unwillingness to part with it. That is how

---

82. Maclaren, *Ezekiel, Daniel, and the Minor Prophets*, 332.
83. Maclaren, *Ezekiel, Daniel, and the Minor Prophets*, 332.
84. Maclaren, *Ezekiel, Daniel, and the Minor Prophets*, 332.
85. Maclaren, *Ezekiel, Daniel, and the Minor Prophets*, 332–33.
86. Maclaren, *Ezekiel, Daniel, and the Minor Prophets*, 333.

they fling bones to dogs. That is not how you have to give your money and your efforts to God and God's cause.[87]

He narrated how farmers mindlessly work on machines to sow seeds. Maclaren argued such a mentality should not be true for Christian giving. A changed attitude toward giving was the second step to generosity.

The final step, according to Maclaren, is give sacrificially. He imagined a fictitious cleaning detergent for his audience. He pictured how this fictitious soap, if it was applied to the church's financial books, would wash away the gifts of all those who did not give sacrificially. He imagined what the finances of the church might look like afterwards. His congregation might find that even some of the biggest donations would be washed away. He powerfully concluded, "God asks how much is kept, not how much is given."[88]

Maclaren then announced his final main point: "One last suggestion I would make on this text is that it brings before us the possible blessing and possible grave results of right or wrong Christian giving."[89] He derived this point from the prophet's rhetorical question in the final clause of the text. He answered the prophet's question by saying a blemished sacrifice would have no chance of receiving help or blessings from the authority figure. Furthermore, the New Testament taught that what was true of giving money was also true of the spiritual life. Maclaren pointed to several passages where Christ used monetary concepts to illustrate spiritual realities.

Maclaren viewed the text as having several theological implications that are still relevant for his hearers. First, generosity changes a Christian's character. He claimed to have seen people who gave generously when they were poor; however, when they found riches, they lost their generous spirit and thus hindered their spiritual growth. In contrast, others treated their newly found wealth as if it was a gift for God, and they grew in the grace and knowledge of Christ. He urged his audience, "Dear friends, God has given all of us something in charge, the faithful use of which is a potent factor in the growth of our Christian characters."[90]

Second, giving influences one's eternal future. He went to both the words of Christ and the words of Paul to show that not only Malachi but

---

87. Maclaren, *Ezekiel, Daniel, and the Minor Prophets*, 334.
88. Maclaren, *Ezekiel, Daniel, and the Minor Prophets*, 335.
89. Maclaren, *Ezekiel, Daniel, and the Minor Prophets*, 335.
90. Maclaren, *Ezekiel, Daniel, and the Minor Prophets*, 336.

also the New Testament taught this concept. Therefore, he appealed to his hearers,

> Let us take care that we do not, in our dread of damaging the free grace of God, forget that although we do not earn blessedness, here or hereafter, by gifts whilst we are living or legacies when we are dead, the administration of money has an important part to play in shaping Christian character, and the Christian character which we acquire here settles our hereafter.[91]

With that application, he moved to the conclusion. The conclusion was very short. He gave one final exhortation to heed the lesson of the text by correctly giving to God and then insisted the text posed an obligation for those listening:

> Brethren! we [sic] all need to revise our scale of giving, especially in regard to missionary operations. And if we will do that at the foot of the Cross, then we shall join the chorus, 'Worthy is the Lamb that was slain to receive *riches*,' and we shall come to Him 'bringing our silver and our gold with us,' rejoicing that He gives us the possibility of sharing His blessedness, 'according to the word of the Lord Jesus which He spake, It is more blessed to give than to receive.'[92]

Maclaren conveyed the spirit of his prophetic text by closing his sermon with this powerful exhortation. Thus, he demonstrated for pastors and teachers how to convey to their audiences the authoritative spirit of the prophetic and epistolary passages.

DISCUSSION QUESTIONS

1. What characteristics make the prophetic and epistolary literature easier to teach than other biblical genres? What characteristics make them more difficult to teach?

2. How did the epistles fulfill a role in the first century similar to the prophets' role before Christ? What similarities are shared between the epistles and the prophets?

3. Try finding text-grounded applications for Ezek 34:1–6, Zech 14, Eph 4:11–14, and 1 Cor 1:26–31.

91. Maclaren, *Ezekiel, Daniel, and the Minor Prophets*, 336–37.
92. Maclaren, *Ezekiel, Daniel, and the Minor Prophets*, 337.

7

Conclusion

"Not his own imagination, nor any fine things of his own spinning.... The more he suppresses himself, and becomes but a voice through which God speaks, the better for himself, his hearers, and his work."

—Alexander Maclaren

Exposition involves explaining the text and applying it to one's audience. Preachers and teachers often mistakenly import significance into Scripture when applications are disconnected from the original author's intended meaning for his text. When it comes to application, we must find a way to bridge the gap between the original author's setting and our own setting. Finding the correct process to move from past hearers to contemporary audiences will enable text-grounded applications that do not cast off authorial intent. Preachers need models that demonstrate appropriate methods of how to make application.

Alexander Maclaren serves as such a model for preachers and teachers. He carefully exegeted the text in order to find its theological lessons and then used these universal truths as bridges to apply the text. The idea that the text's theological lesson can help drive application is not a new concept for homileticians. Maclaren's genius was not in inventing a new method of application but in modeling consistently how to use theology to appropriately apply God's Word. He was one of the most popular and prolific preachers of the Victorian era partially due to his ability to apply the Bible relevantly to his hearers.

Maclaren's methodology did not develop in a vacuum. Numerous individuals influenced him as he developed his philosophy of preaching. The events and people of Maclaren's life shaped his theology of the preacher and preaching practice. He first saw the preacher as an evangelist whose task was to preach the gospel and bring people to Christ. Second, the preacher is a teacher, charged with explaining and stewarding the Word of God to his congregation. Third, the preacher is a herald who stands as God's representative and calls people to follow the Lord. Fourth, the preacher's life and sermons must be centered on Christ. Without Christ's power in the pastor and in the moment, the message will fail. Finally, the preacher must make text-grounded application to his audience. It does little to simply state what a text meant; we must drive home the practical meaning of the text to our hearers.

Of these five emphases, this work focused on the latter. Maclaren's sermons are characterized by applications grounded in the text. He said a preacher

> has to direct the searchlight on individual sins, especially those prevalent in the class form whom his hearer are [sic] drawn. He has to apply the measure of the sanctuary to worldly maxims which his hearers take for axioms, and to practices which they think legitimate because they are popular. . . . The true church must always be remonstrant, protestant, a standing rebuke to the world, till the world has accepted and applied the principles of the Gospel to personal and social life. And the preacher who does not give voice to the church's protest fails in one of his plainest and chiefest duties.[1]

He attempted to give practical applications to his congregation that were grounded in a careful exegesis of the text in the original language. This commitment made him stand out from other preachers in his day.[2] Maclaren used his exegesis to find the universal truths that the biblical author wanted to convey. Since the theology of the text does not change despite time or audience, Maclaren treated the theology as a bridge to create relevant applications that were consistent with authorial intent.

---

1. Maclaren, "Old Preacher on Preaching," 36.
2. Wilkinson, *Modern Masters of Pulpit Discourse*, 124.

This understanding of Maclaren's preaching philosophy lays the groundwork for properly analyzing his sermons. Maclaren believed the narratives were accurate descriptions of historical events. However, the authors' purposes were not simply to record history but to convey theological lessons. Maclaren exegeted the text in order to find these lessons in the stories, and since these lessons were true for both the original audience and his congregation, he used the theology to help him craft applications that were relevant but also text-appropriate.

While this general method of applying a passage can be useful for preachers in the twenty-first century, three qualities of his sermons from the narratives are especially helpful. First, he used the theological lesson of the text to show how the original readers shared much in common with contemporary Christians. These common experiences can help preachers find situations today where the same theological lessons likewise apply. Second, he showed how to study the characters to find applications. The main point of the text is to teach theology; however, the characters can provide clues for how followers of God should respond to the theological message of the story. Third, he demonstrated the benefits of vividly retelling the story. Retelling the biblical narratives can help the audience identify with both the characters in the story and the original readers. Once this happens, the audience can see more clearly how the passage applies to them.

Likewise, preachers can look at his sermons from Deuteronomy and Leviticus to glean insights on how to apply biblical law. Maclaren believed the law was rooted in Israel's relationship to God under the old covenant; nevertheless, he treated the law as still applicable to Christians because the statues and instructions were written in order to teach the Israelites universal truths. Progressive revelation proved that these theological ideas still hold true for Christians even if the law itself had been fulfilled in Christ. Thus, his applications from the law were grounded in the author's theological purpose for the text.

Expository preachers and teachers can learn four lessons from Maclaren's sermons on the law. First, the law should be interpreted in its original context. It was written for Israelites under the old covenant; therefore, applications should be grounded in what the text meant for them before asking its relevance for Christians. Second, applications should be tied to the theology of the text rather than an evaluation of the law as being civil, ceremonial, or moral. Since the biblical author intended for the law to convey theological truths, the theology behind the law becomes a more solid grounds for application than segregating laws artificially into civil, ceremonial, or moral categories. Third, applications should come from a careful analysis of the historical setting and literary context. The law was instituted to apply a principle of Scripture to a specific, concrete issue Israel faced. This should not cause pastors to shy away from biblical law but rather should motivate them to discover how the same theological principle is still concretely applicable in similar situations today. Fourth, applications ought to be concrete and functional and not simply soteriological. Although Maclaren connected the law to Christ, he did not make the acceptance of Christ his only application from the law. He found similar situations in his day where the theological principle appeared and urged his audience to obey the text in those situations. In these ways, his method of application can serve as a model for applying the law.

Similarly, Maclaren can serve as a model for applying the psalms. He believed the psalms functioned to "echo" the spirit of the law. They are divinely inspired human prayers about God to God. Maclaren thus exegeted the text in order to find these theological lessons. He connected the theological truths taught by the psalmists to his audience. He argued he was warranted to make such applications from the psalms because Christians today share the same faith in God as the psalmists did.

Maclaren illustrated two practices of applying the psalms that can be especially helpful for preachers and teachers. First, he frequently pointed out how the psalmists' emotions were still felt by people in his day. If people can connect to the emotion within the psalm, then the relevance of the psalm becomes more illuminating to them. Second, he argued that the psalmists' responses to God demonstrate how Christians ought to respond to God correctly in their own lives. The theological grounds for the psalmists' prayers are still true for Christians; therefore, he found similar situations in his time that were analogous to the setting of the original author. This means of applying the book of Psalms can help preachers understand how to apply the book to their own congregations.

The same can be said of his preaching from the wisdom literature. He believed biblical wisdom was founded upon theological truths. Since wisdom is theologically driven, the relevance of biblical wisdom only becomes clear when one draws near to God. Even though the wisdom books on the surface appear to be man-centered, they are actually God-centered.

Maclaren altered his approach in the wisdom literature depending on the book from which he was preaching. He argued the book of Proverbs showed how to live wisely. Job and Ecclesiastes, on the other hand, tell the story of humanity's search for true wisdom. Consequently, individual verses from Job and Ecclesiastes may on the surface appear true if the interpreter fails to connect them to the book's overall message. One should also include the rest of the canon of Scripture to see how progressive revelation has developed the topic further.

Maclaren's sermons from the wisdom books demonstrate several lessons for preachers to take away. First, focus on the God-centered nature of biblical wisdom, and use progressive revelation to help make text-appropriate applications. Keeping the focus on God and theology can prevent sermons from sounding purely like a lesson on good morals. Second, use illustrations and stories to apply the message of the text because they help people see how the wisdom of the text connects to their own situations. Furthermore, since young people were the primary audiences of the original authors, consider taking some time to address them directly when preaching from the wisdom. Third, connect the wisdom passage to both Christ and contemporary circumstances. On the one hand, Christ is the source of wisdom, so preachers should not neglect the gospel from the wisdom, but on the other hand, wisdom is intended to be practical. Sermon applications must balance both qualities. Fourth, when in Ecclesiastes or Job, demonstrate the importance of looking to both the immediate context and the New Testament for insight. In these ways, Maclaren can be a great help to expositors as they try to navigate the wisdom literature.

Finally, Maclaren's method of application can benefit preachers when studying the prophetic and epistolary books. Maclaren believed the prophets and epistles shared much in common. For example, like how the prophets applied the Torah to the people, the epistles exposited the implications of the gospel for the church. Moreover, Maclaren understood how both the prophets and epistles were written to address specific historical contexts. The authors denounced the sins their audiences faced and revealed how hope ultimately comes from God's grace through repentance and faith.

Preachers can take away from Maclaren three lessons on how to apply the prophets and epistles. First, applications must be based on a proper exegesis of the text in its historical and literary context. Only after first understanding the authors in their original context can preachers then find appropriate situations to which the text can be applied. Second, focus on the unchanging nature of human sinfulness and the character of God. The specific ways a sin appeared in the Israelite society or the early church may not be prevalent anymore, but the sin itself still rears its head in analogous situations today. Therefore, preachers and teachers need to reveal how the sin problem in the text still affects contemporary individuals and society. Third, connect your applications to the person and works of Christ. Every text has an implied hope of God's grace conditioned on people's repentance. Maclaren correctly showed how this hope is true through faith in Christ alone.

In summary, Alexander Maclaren's method of applying a biblical passage involved carefully exegeting the text to find the theology the author meant to convey. He believed these lessons were true for all people despite place, culture, or time, thus he used the author's theology as a bridge to find applications that were text-grounded but also relevant for his audience. He followed this process of application regardless of where his text was found in God's Word. Therefore, Maclaren can serve as a model for expositors today for how to craft text-driven applications that are bound to authorial intent and yet practical and specific to listeners today.

His call to preachers and teachers in his day consequently needs to resonate in the ears of expositors still:

> The word rendered 'preach' is instructive. It means 'to cry' and suggests the manner befitting those who bear God's message. They should sound it out loudly, plainly, urgently, with earnestness and marks of emotion in their voice. Languid whispers will not wake sleepers. Unless the messenger is manifestly in earnest, the message will fall flat. Not with bated breath, as if ashamed of it; nor with hesitation, as if not quite sure of it; nor with coolness, as if it were of little urgency, is God's Word to be pealed in men's ears. The preacher is a crier.[3]

May those entrusted to apply God's Word to the church today feel that same God-given urgency.

DISCUSSION QUESTIONS

1. Why is it important to find the theological purpose of a text before crafting application? How does theology form an appropriate bridge between exegesis and application?
2. After reading this book, what do you feel was Maclaren's greatest contribution to the field of biblical application?

3. Maclaren, *Ezekiel, Daniel, and the Minor Prophets*, 190–91.

3. How should your applications change depending on the genre from which a passage is found? How did Maclaren's sermons demonstrate a sensitivity to the biblical genres?

Appendix

"An Old Preacher on Preaching"[1]

FACT AND LOGIC ARE both outraged by the names of the two Unions which join in this assembly. The division into Congregationalists and Baptists is faulty as if one said, Englishmen and Londoners, for all Baptists are Congregationalists. We are closest of kin among the Free Churches, and perhaps, therefore, have sometimes been furthest apart, for cordiality often increases as the square of the distance. But we all feel the influence of the uniting tendency which is so marked a feature of the present time, and of which we are happy in seeing with us to-day a distinguished representative in the person of my old school-fellow and present friend, the first Moderator of the United Free Church of Scotland. Our joint meetings do but demonstrate, on a somewhat larger scale, our relations in most cases all through the country. They are the natural expression of a real and felt unity, not a hollow show of an unreal. I sometimes venture to think that the ministers of the two Churches are in more cordial and closer relations than their flocks are. But be that as it may, we all meet to-day as brethren with

---

1. This lecture is used with kind permission of the Angus Library and Archive at Regent's Park College, Oxford. It is recorded in *Report of the Joint Assembly of the Baptist and Congregational Unions, April 23 and 25, 1901: With Illustrative Notes*. 19–40. London: Baptist Tract and Book Society, 1901. Maclaren was seventy-five years old when he preached this message. It is one of the last speeches he delivered outside Union Chapel, and he passed away almost exactly nine years later.

hearty goodwill and mutual sympathy, and I esteem it a signal honour to occupy the place which I do, on so happy an occasion.

In casting about for a topic for this address, I have thought of many burning questions which it would be timely to discuss, but I feel it wisest to keep to my own *métier*. I am a preacher, and have been for more than half a century; I speak here mainly to preachers, and I venture to offer some considerations as to the preacher's office, its themes, its demands, its possibilities. No one will deny that the question of whether our preaching is as efficacious as it might be is a burning question, too. Widespread searchings of heart are at work among the Free Churches on that matter. And they have only too good ground in the contrast which would strike us as alarming if we were not so accustomed to it, between the immense amount of effort and the small results apparent. I suppose there are some 6,000 or 8,000 sermons delivered every Sunday by the ministers of our two denominations—and what comes of them all? We have covered the land with chapels, and yet do we even keep up with the growth of population? "Ye have sowed much, and brought home little;" and if so much seed yields so scanty a harvest, the sower may well ask himself, Why? No doubt there are trends of thought and habits of life to-day which make the preacher's task eminently hard; but we have no such difficulties to face as the first messengers of the Cross had to encounter and overcame. Are the philosophical or scientific tendencies of to-day worse than the front which wisdom-seeking Greece presented to them? Are the habits of to-day more antagonistic to the gospel than was the corruption that honeycombed the luxurious sensualism of Asia? Is the secularising influence of trade and imperialism more hostile than was the self-centred pride of Rome, with its cult of the Emperor? Is the ignorance of our slums more dense than the darkness that wrapped "the regions beyond"? And yet the Message conquered. Why not now? The Message is the same; the Divine power that clothed the messengers is the same. "O thou that art named the house of Israel, is the Spirit of the Lord straitened? are these His doings?" Surely there can be but one answer to the twofold question—an answer which throws us back on ourselves, and bids us look to ourselves as the causes of the loss of power. The last character in which I should desire to stand before brethren whom I honour so highly and love so much, is that of an accuser. But I have nearly finished my work, and I would fain use the opportunity given me to-day, to leave some words which my younger brethren, whose task promises to be still more difficult than that of us older men, may perhaps feel to derive some additional weight, because they may be the last which the speaker will address to such an assembly. If I venture to speak of the preacher and his work, I must lay bare my own ideals, and to do that is to lay bare my own shortcomings, for our ideals are the sternest critics of our accomplishments.

It may be freely admitted that the preacher, as the Free Churches know him, is the result of a process of evolution starting with the simple New Testament arrangements. Whether the process has been legitimate, and the product satisfactory, or whether there are further developments to be expected and desired, need not concern us now. The point which I seek to make is that, whilst great authorities have told us that differentiation of functions is the mark of progressive evolution, we have in the preacher of to-day an apparent coalescence of three offices which are separate in the early Church—those of evangelist, teacher and prophet. I purpose to deal with my subject under these three points of view.

The preacher is, first and foremost, an evangelist—a bearer of good news. The very name contains a designation of the preacher's theme, for it, at least, makes this clear—that he has to tell a fact, which is full freighted with gladness for a sad world. Whatever more the gospel is, it is primarily the history of something that did occur. The far-reaching presuppositions and implications of the fact, its force as the spring of transformed humanity, of individual and social progress, open out into a wide room where all speculative and practical intellects may expatiate, but the beginning of all these is a Person and the fact of His life and death. The grain of mustard seed grows into the great tree in whose branches all the birds can nest and sing, beneath whose shadow all the peoples can house. "We preach Christ crucified." It is one thing to preach salvation by Christ; it is another to preach Christ as the Saviour. The more we can free ourselves from the abstract and technical theology of the schools, and can make our words throb with the miracle of that loving, human heart, and with the pathos and power of that death for a world's sins, the more shall we deserve the name of evangelists. Hearts are more surely to be won by showing them Jesus crucified than by our comments on the sight. A Christ without a cross is a king without a throne. If our ministry is to have power, it must all centre in the Death for the world's sins. Otherwise it will be like a lighthouse without a lamp. It will have no grip, no impulse, no regenerating power. "I, if I be lifted up, will draw all men." There are preachers who demagnetise the gospel, because they falter in the proclamation of that "lifting up" which, because it is the secret of Christ's power to heal the fiery serpent's poisoned sting is the secret of His power to draw, first, the languid looks of the victims, and then their whole nature, yielded to Him in love and loyalty. The experience of the recent Free Church Missions taught us all that, when we really "meant business" and were seeking for what would touch hearts, we instinctively went back to the simple elementary truths which some of us had been tempted to think too simple and elementary for our intelligent audiences, or too threadbare to be listened to with interest. When preachers really and intensely desire to "save souls,"—and have found that that old-fashioned phrase has a meaning to-day—they will instinctively grasp the only instrument that can effect the purpose, and will find themselves saying: "This is a faithful saying, and worthy of all acceptation, that Jesus Christ came into the world to save sinners,"—and they will be wise if they add with Paul "of whom I am chief," for the sense of personal need is an indispensable element in the evangelist's work.

Our message implies that sin is a universal reality, from which there is no deliverance but through Jesus. Has the fact of sin, its reality and its consequences, its due place in modern preaching? I for one very much doubt it. Modern theories of heredity and environment, modern laxity of moral fibre have taken many shades of blackness out of the black thing. Men think less gravely of sin, and so they superficially diagnose the world's disease, and therefore they superficially prescribe the remedy. An inadequate conception of sin lies at the root of most theological heresies and Utopian schemes of reformation of society. It is fatal to the earnestness, the pathos and the power of the preacher's work. Unless we have our hearts and minds laden with the burden of men's sins, our voices will not ring out the vibrating notes of the good news of One who saves His people from their sins, because "Himself bare our sins in His own body." We must all confess that, yielding to the "Zeitgeist," the trend of opinion and feeling prevalent around us, and as children of the age, we have been tempted to think less severely, less pityingly of sin, and less solemnly of its certain result, death, than either our Master or His apostles did. We have too much shrunk from plain speech on the guilt and the danger of sinners. And, just in exact proportion to our failure in these respects has necessarily followed our failure in ringing out the good news of the Christ, the propitiation for our sins and for the whole world.

The preacher is further spoken of in the New Testament as a herald, and that title implies that his proclamation be plain, clear, assured. He is not to speak timidly, as if diverse winds of doctrine had blown back his voice into his trumpet. He is not to bring an ambiguous message in cloudy words. "O thou that tellest good tidings to Zion, lift up thy voice with strength; lift it up, be not afraid." The evangelist needs to deliver his good news with urgency, as if it was of some moment that people should know and accept it. Is that note of urgency audible, as it should be, in our preaching? The evangelist has need of tenderness. "We entreat as though God did beseech by us." What outgush of sympathetic yearning can be too great fitly to bear on its current the message of a love which died to save? Are we not too little accustomed to preach with our hearts? Should we not be foolishly ashamed to say, "I now tell you, even weeping?" The evangelist has need of the personal element in his message. It has to be rigidly subordinated, else he is in danger of preaching himself, not Jesus. He has not to obtrude his own personality, but he has to speak as one who has felt the rapture of the joyful news which he proclaims. "We have found the Messiah," was the first Christian sermon ever preached, and it was so efficacious that it converted the whole congregation, for it brought Peter to Jesus. "That which we have seen and handled, that proclaim we unto you" is the mould into which the most effectual evangelising work has ever run. The evangelist has need of elasticity in his methods, while he preserves uniformity in his theme. Our recent Mission has taught us that, if we are to get at the outlying masses, whom the Church of to-day, thank God! is awakening to long to reach, we must not be afraid of flinging away some of our old appliances, and shaping new ways of getting at the dense crowds of English heathens. Our stereotyped services do not attract them, and never will. Personally I do not believe that "the masses" will ever be reached, until Christian men and women, in far larger numbers and with far more system than hitherto, go among them, and by individual effort cast silken chains of sympathy and brotherliness round them which may draw them out of the depths. But we must also have changes in methods, and the abandonment of a stiff conservatism which would fossilise our churches. I am not pleading for anything sensational, still less for importing entertainments either for eye or ear into our evangelistic work. All I wish to emphasise is that we must vary our methods, and take care that the eternal freshness of the ever young Good News is not hidden under the mustiness of ancient modes of action, which have proved to be ineffectual to reach the multitudes of "them that are without."

But the preacher has to be a teacher as well as an evangelist. Whether it is a development in accordance with the principles of the New Testament Church that all public, oral teaching should be in his hands is a question that does not concern us here. We may freely allow that a higher ideal would be: "When ye come together, each one hath a psalm, hath a teaching, hath a revelation," and yet see that the present order of things is best for the present spiritual state of the Church, and be sure that as soon as that changes for the better, the old order will change with it. When the temperature rises, there will be an outburst of spring flowers.

But the teaching office of the preacher is depreciated, not only in the name of an appeal to the primitive condition of the Church, but from the extreme other side of the most modern outlook on things, as being superseded by the hundred-voiced Press. The men and women of this generation, we are told, form their opinions from books, not from sermons. I should demur to the word "form," as expressing the process by which a large proportion of them arrive at what they call their opinions; I should consent to say "get their opinions," for it is not a process of reasoned formation, but of more or less accidental and unreasoned acquisition. The opinions do not grow, are not shaped by patient labour, but are imported into the new owner's mind ready made, "in Germany," or elsewhere, but certainly not in his own workshop. But granting the influence of the press, if it supersedes the pulpit, it is the fault of the occupant thereof. A certain minister once told a shrewd old Scottish lady that he was engaged to deliver an address on the power of the pulpit, and asked what her views on the subject were. She answered, "The power o' the pulpit! That depends on wha's in it." Which is a truth to be laid to heart by all preachers. No man is superseded but through his own deficiencies. There must be weakness in the wall which the storm blows down. The living voice has all its old power to-day, when it is a voice, and not an echo, or a mumble. If a man has anything to say and will say it with all his heart and with all his soul and with all his strength, he will not lack auditors. Books have their province and preachers have theirs, and neither can efface the other or supply the place of the other. The cry that the pulpit is effete comes mostly from quarters which do not despise the pulpit so much as dislike the truths which it teaches only too powerfully for their liking.

We may, then, turn to consider that aspect of the preacher's work undisturbed. And the first thing that I desire to lay stress on is, that the educational is never to be separated from the evangelistic office. True, "there are diversities of operations;" and idiosyncracies and spiritual gifts, which for the most part follow in their line, may mark out one man more especially for the one kind of work, and another for the other. We must all rejoice that there are brethren among us who are endowed with remarkable gifts of presenting the Good News, which clearly disclose Christ's purpose for them. Still, it remains true and important to keep in view, that the truest teaching must be evangelistic, and the truest evangelising must be educational. The web is made up of warp and woof. The evangelism which appeals to emotion only is false to the gospel; for God's way of moving men is to bring truth to their understandings, which shall then set their emotions at work, and so pass on to move the will, the directress of the man, and thus at last affect the actions. As Whichcote says, "Religion begins with knowledge; it proceeds to temper, and ends in practice." The evangelist who is not a teacher will build nothing that will last. And not less one-sided, and therefore transient, will be the work of the teacher who is not an evangelist. He will give husks instead of the bread of life, notions that may rattle in skulls like seeds in dried poppyheads, but not convictions which burn all the more because they are light as well as heat.

The true theologian ever brings his doctrines to bear on the emotions, and then on the will, and then on practice. That "theology" suffers under the imputation of being abstract, dry, remote from life is the fault of the teacher, not of the subject. The preacher is not to duplicate his part, like an actor who sustains two characters in a play, and to come on the stage in one scene as evangelist, and in another as teacher. He is to be both at once and to be both always.

For the most advanced instruction that can be given or received does not leave the most initial truths behind. It only unfolds them. The teacher's subject-matter is the same as the evangelist's. The difference lies in the mode of viewing it, and the purpose for which it is considered. The last book of Euclid rests on the axioms and postulates that precede the first. No Christian thought can ever travel beyond the Incarnation, Sacrifice, and Ascension of Jesus Christ, the Indwelling Spirit, "the forgiveness of sins and the life everlasting." To leave these behind is not progress but decadence. Not to get past, but to get more deeply into, these truths is the growth of the Christian life. Bees press themselves down into the flowers from which they would draw the honey, "and murmur by the hour" in their bells. Wasps and other vagrant things flit past them and get none. "Whoever goeth onward"—as John says, with a flash of irony as he quotes the advanced thinker's watchword—"and abideth not in the teaching of Christ, hath not God." The reminder would benefit some modern successors of those proud, old incipient Gnostics. To lead minds to see the profound and far-reaching truths that underlie the gospel, what its facts presuppose of God and Man, of the Father and the Eternal Word, what they reveal of the heart of things, and of the Heart at the heart of them; to lead to the recognition, and still more to the application to individual and social and national life, of the principles that flow from the facts; to disclose to the minds and to lay on the hearts of men the Incarnation and Sacrifice and Reign of Jesus as the world-redeeming power, as the revelation of the perfect life for men and nations; to find and exhibit in Jesus, the answer to all the questions of the intellect, the satisfaction of all the needs of the heart, the source and standard of ethics, the fountain of all wisdom, the renovator of humanity, the purifier of society, the King of Men—and to keep fast by the Cross and Passion of that Lord, while He is following out the issues of His work to their remotest consequences—these are the tasks of the Christian preacher in his capacity of teacher. All knowledge may come into his sphere. There is room for the widest culture. The teacher may elaborate his theme with the closest thought, or may adorn it with poetry and imagination. There is room for all gifts in the building of the great temple. Bezaleel was taught by the Spirit of God to execute his works of artistic beauty, and Hiram's workmen had to hew logs in Lebanon. But the wider the teacher sweeps his circle, the stronger must be its centre. The more he lengthens his cords, the more must he strengthen his stakes,—and the middle prop that holds up the tent is the Cross with Christ upon it. "Him first, Him last, Him midst and without end." All that the teacher has to teach is summed up in one word—Christ. His whole theme is "the truth as it is in Jesus."

As the theme is Christ, so the text-book is the Bible. Whatever the Higher Criticism has done, it has not touched the main substance of the gospel which we have to preach, nor do even its most advanced positions seem to me seriously to affect the homiletic worth of Scripture. The truths of the Bible remain, even if extreme theories as to date and manner of origination of its several parts were much more undeniably proven than they are. I venture to use the privilege of age and appeal very earnestly to my younger brethren especially, beseeching them not to be tempted by either the mistaken notion of increasing the attractiveness of their preaching, or by the natural wish of youth to do something original and break away from conventions. Conventional usages were instinct with life and meaning when they were new, and it is best to try whether their original significance is worth saving before we resolve to shake them off. The habit of prefacing a sermon with a text is, no doubt, a survival, and it is sometimes unmeaning enough; but it is a witness that the sermon's true purpose is to explain, confirm, and enforce Scripture. Once the text was followed by a sermon dealing with it. Would that it were always so now! Better to put new life into the old form by making a text really what it is meant to be, than to break through it in a flight after something "fresh and unconventional."

It does not follow from the Bible's being the text-book that preaching is to be expository in the technical sense of that word, though I confess to a belief that if we had more of that we should have a robuster type of Christian, with a firmer grip of his professed creed, than is common today. The days of protracted exposition are, for good or evil, over. There will be no more courses of sermons like those which the painful and reverend Mr. Caryll perpetrated on Job, and published in three thick folios—double-columned, if my memory is correct.

The widest scope is to be given to varieties of mind and ways of assimilating Scripture; but that ministry only is true to its duties, and up to the height of its large possibilities, which makes its main purpose the drawing out into clear statement, and the supporting by forceful argument, and the impressing by emotional pleadings, what it has pleased God to say to men. If it was worth His while to give us the Book, it is worth our while to toil to fathom its depth, to saturate our thinking and feeling with its truths, and it is our highest function and office to interpret them to our brethren. We shall "shine as lights in the world" if we "hold forth the Word of Life." There are nebulae, as well as brilliant stars, in the firmament of the Word. It is for the preacher to show men that the stars are suns, and the nebulae galaxies of light. How unworthy it is for him to direct his telescope from the heaven of the Word to the low levels of current topics! I shall have to speak presently of the place which the latter must hold in the preacher's work; but they will hold their right place only if he is true to his vocation as being first of all a minister of the Word of God.

More reasons than can be enumerated, much less expanded here, concur in enforcing this. In no other profession would the text-books be treated as the Bible sometimes is. There is no such discipline for the preacher as the careful, minute study of Scripture. Patient work with such unspiritual implements as lexicon and concordance yields rich fruits of spiritual discernment, gives such grasp of great principles as nothing else will give, opens out endless vistas into the deep things of God, as witness such books as the Bishop of Durham's priceless commentaries on John and Hebrews. A preacher who has steeped himself in the Bible will have a clearness of outlook which will illuminate many dark things, and a firmness of touch which will breed confidence in him among his hearers. He will have the secret of perpetual freshness, for he cannot exhaust the Bible. No pulpit teaching will last as long as that which is given honestly and persistently to the elucidation and enforcement of Biblical truth. As the Scotch psalm-book has it:

> "In old age, when others fade
> He fruit still forth shall bring."

We have to do the work of Christian teachers under remarkable conditions. On the one hand there is great ignorance of Scripture and of systematised Christian truth among our congregations, and we are perpetually in danger of overestimating the amount of knowledge on which we may reckon. Otherwise well-educated men and women have but the vaguest notions as to Scripture facts and the most confused apprehensions of Christian ideas. I for one believe that a considerable percentage in every congregation in the land is unaffected by our sermons because it does not understand what we are saying. We have to aim at simplicity, not to be afraid of being elementary, and to say as Paul said, "To write the same things to you, to me indeed is not grievous and for you it is safe." On the other hand, we have to speak to people who have considerable education, and some who think they have more than they really have, who have been fed on a miscellaneous collection of scraps, *De omnibus rebus—et quibusdam aliis*, in magazines and handbooks, and it is hard to get an entrance for solid Christian truth into such minds. Short sermons, this Sunday's having no connection with last Sunday's, and based on snippets of Scripture, the meaning of which is of small consequence, correspond to the week's diet of desultory reading. And withal there is the heaving swell of intellectual unrest, which affects all our congregations. How are we to discharge our teaching work in the face of all this?

Mainly by the strong, sympathetic presentation of positive truth. Controversy is needful, but it is seldom efficacious. It convinces the already convinced. Better to abound in affirmations than in negations, though they will be branded as dogmatism. Speak the truth, as you know it and feel it, and let it work. There are two ways of getting rid of weeds—to grub them up, or to sow good seed, which will spring and clear the ground. And we must never forget that what we have to teach is no philosophy for the few, no system of doctrine for trained understandings, but the gospel for the world. When one of Luther's disciples once asked him for some guidance as to how he

"An Old Preacher on Preaching"

should preach before the Duke, the Doctor said, "All your sermons should be of the simplest. Do not regard the prince, but the simple, stupid, rude, and unlearned people, who are cut out of the same cloth as the prince. If, in my sermon, I were to have Philip Melancthon and the other doctors in my eye, I should produce nothing good; but I preach in the simplest way to the unlearned, and it suits everybody." Some of our hearers are educated and can follow our highest flights, but many of them cannot. But all have the one human heart, with its deepest needs identical in all. Sad souls are to be comforted, torpid ones to be stung or startled or wooed into sensitiveness and activity, eyes glued to earth to be drawn to look up, the inmost self, which is ever in its depths lonely, to be led to the Immortal Companion and lover of all souls, the consciousness of the bondage and burden of sin to be roused, and, when roused, to be soothed—and the preacher is to do all this! Surely the vision of the needs of a gathered audience might strike the most eloquent dumb, and make the most confident timid. But "our sufficiency is of God," and God's sufficiency will be ours, in the measure in which we steadfastly follow out the purpose of making our preaching truly Biblical. If we draw from these deep fountains we shall never return with our vessels empty.

The preacher's work has a third aspect. Besides being evangelistic and educational it is also ethical, and, in that aspect especially, may rightly be designated as Prophetic. Of course the form of "inspiration" belonging to the prophet in Israel is not claimed for the Christian prophet, but every true preacher should be able to say, Thus saith the Lord, and if we do not speak what we have heard in the ear in many a secret "hour of high communion with the living God" we had better be silent for evermore. It may be objected that the preacher has neither the inspiration nor the insight into the future which belonged to the prophet. But there are different forms of inspiration; and that which is secured by hours of communion, by earnest effort to stretch the narrow tablet of the mind so that it shall be capacious enough to hold the amplitude of God's message, by sedulous suppression of our own clamorous opinions and resolute turning a deaf ear to the world's noises, by docility and by prayer, is no less real than that which touched Isaiah's with a live coal. "There are diversities of gifts, but the same Spirit." Philip the evangelist's seven daughters, or the prophets in the Corinthian Church, had no inspiration which we have not. What does Paul direct as to the latter? "Let them speak by two or three, and let the others *discern*," a function which is very cheerfully and abundantly discharged among us. So the New Testament prophet's teaching had to submit to criticism. It had further to submit sometimes to being cut short; "If a revelation be made to another standing by, let the first keep silence." So a New Testament prophet could be tedious and had to learn to give way. There seems no reason to believe that the inspiration which endowed these prophets has ceased to be given to us. Much rather is it that the name has become disused, than that the persons who have a right to it have failed. Are there not Prophets among us to-day? Have there not always been Prophets in the Church?

Nor does the lack of the predictive insight damage the claim to the name. It is a commonplace now that that element is not the sole, nor even the principal, one in the ideal of the prophet. If we rightly understand what he was to Israel we shall rightly understand how he still survives, in modern garb indeed, but the same. For his chief function was to be an incarnation of the national conscience. It was his task to hold aloft the Divine Ideal for Israel, to bring life to the test of the Divine law, to stand before king and people undismayed, with his face as iron against their faces, to denounce national and individual transgression, to set the trumpet to his "mouth and declare to Israel its sin." He was necessarily a predicter, not only because God gave to some of the order a foreknowledge of particular events, but also because God had graven deep in his mind the sure conviction that righteousness exalts a nation, that all national or individual departure from God is bitter as well as evil, that sin is death, and good the sure result in the long run of goodness. The prophet supplied the force for the Law, the dynamic by which it got itself obeyed. As one of them says, his word was "as a hammer," to drive home and fasten in a sure place the nails of the Law.

And is not this the function of the Christian Church as a whole, and eminently of its preachers? What are we here for but to bring the principles of the gospel to bear on all life? No doubt the courtiers of an Ahab or a Zedekiah said what they thought clever things about the fastidious prophetic conscience, just as we have heard would-be taunts which were really tributes and turned to a testimony, about "the Nonconformist conscience." It is the Christian conscience, and to be its voice is no small part of the preacher's duty. He has to direct the searchlight on individual sins, especially those prevalent in the class from whom his hearers are drawn. He has to apply the measure of the sanctuary to worldly maxims which his hearers take for axioms, and to practices which they think legitimate because they are popular. He has to witness against the cancerous vices which are eating out the life of the nation. He has to bring national acts to the standard of Christ's teaching, and to insist that politics is but Christian principles applied to national life. A church which has ceased to protest against the "world," suits the world's purpose exactly, and is really a bit of the world under another name. The true Church must always be remonstrant, protestant, a standing rebuke to the world, till the world has accepted and applied the principles of the gospel to personal and social life. And the preacher who does not give voice to the Church's protest fails in one of his plainest and chiefest duties.

We need brave men in the pulpit, who shall speak with freedom what they believe they have learned from God, of the evils in the land. We need men who have heard Him saying to them, "Be not dismayed *at* them, lest I dismay thee *before* them." We need for the prophet's office much secluded fellowship with God, who "wakens" His servant's "ear morning by morning," and gives them "the tongue of them that are taught." We need to keep clear of popular currents of thought and practice, suspecting always that truth does not dwell with majorities, and that what the multitude acclaim God is likely to condemn. We have to be keenly sensitive to the drift of thought, else we shall not wisely make head against it, or know how to use or direct it. We have to remember that preaching may be as accurately adapted to the times, when it directly contradicts popular dicta, as when it falls in with them, and that the Greeks' demand for wisdom, and the Jews' for a sign, were met by being refused in appearance, even while granted in truth.

We have need to remember the woes pronounced on two classes of prophets—those who "stole the word every man from his neighbour," and those who "prophesied out of their own hearts, having seen nothing" and heard no voice from on high. So we have to be sure that we stand on our own feet, see with our own eyes, are not plagiarists or copyists, nor borrow oil from our neighbours' vessels, but go to them that sell for ourselves. And on the other hand we have to see that the word, which is in that sense our own, is, in a deeper sense, not our own, but God's. We have to deal at first hand with Him, and to suppress self that He may speak. And no man will ever be the Lord's prophet, however eloquent or learned he may be, unless he knows what it is to sit silent before God, and in the silence to hear the still, small, most mighty voice that penetrates the soul, and to the hearing ear is sweet as harpers harping with their harps, and louder than the noise of many waters.

But this prophetic or ethical aspect of the preacher's work can never be rightly done, unless it is based upon the evangelistic and the educational.

Appendix

We shall rejoice that the pulpit and the Church have recognised more clearly than before the call to make their voice heard on Christ's side, in regard to drunkenness, gambling, impurity, and other national vices. But it will be no gain to the cause of Christian morality or of national righteousness, if the ethical side of religion is presented exclusively or disproportionately to the other two, which are its foundation. Let us have applied Christianity by all means—the more the better; but let us make sure first that there is the Christianity to apply. Let us preach Christ as the regenerator of society; but let us not omit to preach Him as the Saviour of the soul from sin. Let us begin where the gospel begins, with "God so loved the world that He gave His only begotten Son, that whosoever believeth in Him should not perish, but have everlasting life,"—and then let us draw forth from the depths of that great word all the teaching which it contains, and all the ethics for single souls, for society and for the world, which flow from it. It is Christ the Sacrifice and the Saviour, who is Christ the wisdom of God, and the realised ideal of humanity, the embodiment of the perfect law for life, the perfect motive to fulfil it, and the perfect giver of the perfect power for obedience. It is Christ, the Sacrifice for men and the wisdom of God, who is the King of nations, from whom the peoples will learn righteousness, and following whom the tribes of the earth shall enter into the land of peace. We, the preachers of His all-transforming and all-vivifying name, have to preach Him in all the aspects of His mission, and to present these, so far as our imperfections will permit, in the order, proportion, and harmony in which they are revealed to us. The threefold beam may be separated into its parts by a prism, but neither of these three is sunshine. The preacher has to try to re-combine them into the sweet, all-blessing white ray, which every eye feels to be light. We are preachers—that is to say, we are evangelists, teachers, prophets. Let us not limit ourselves to either function, but try always to blend the three in that one which should include them all.

Fathers and brethren, I am but too conscious of the imperfection of the conceptions of our office, which I have ventured to lay before you. I am still more conscious of the imperfection of my presentation of these. I am most of all conscious of the imperfections of my attempts at realising their ideal, in my day of service on which the evening shadows are falling. But, however condemnatory may be the light of an ideal of our office, the absence or dimness of that light is fatal. The more loftily we think of our work, the more lowly will be our estimate of ourselves, and the more earnest our efforts to reach up to the height of our possibilities, which are therefore our duties. The more we feel the burden of the Lord laid on us as evangelists, the more shall we have a passion for souls, which will fill our hearts with wistful tenderness, and soften our voices into prevalent entreaty. The more we rise to the requirements of our function as teachers, the more shall we labour to learn what we have to teach, and make all our culture however wide, all our acquirements however various, all our thinking however profound, subservient to the Master Truth, like mirrors set round a central light. And we shall feed the lambs as well as the sheep, the babes as well as the full-grown men, seeking to achieve the simplicity in which full comprehension of deep truths is ever garbed, and so will speak with the authority of the Truth itself and not as the scribes. The more we are constrained by the word of the Lord given to us as His prophets, the more bold shall we be to weigh popular habits and customary sins in the balances of the sanctuary, and the more shall we sometimes be honoured to help in stemming evil—but if not, we shall have delivered our souls, and "whether men will hear or whether they will forbear, they shall know that there hath been a prophet among them."

Some of us are almost passing from the stage, some of us are pressing on to it, eager, hopeful, perhaps thinking that we shall do much better than did the veterans, who now seem to "lag superfluous." The modes of thinking change as do the thinkers, the wonderful new lamps of one age become the dim twinkling candles of the next. Much in our conceptions of the Truth will not long outlive ourselves. That which can be shaken will be removed. Be it so; that which cannot be shaken will remain—and what cannot be shaken is the gospel of the "kingdom that cannot be moved," and its King, the same yesterday, today, and for ever. "All flesh is as grass, and all the glory thereof as the flower of grass. The grass withereth, and the flower falleth: but the word of the Lord abideth for ever. And this is the word which by the gospel is preached."

Bibliography

Akin, Daniel L. "Applying a Text-Driven Sermon." In *Text-Driven Preaching: God's Word at the Heart of Every Sermon*, edited by Daniel L. Akin, David L. Allen, and Ned L. Mathews, 269–93. Nashville: B&H Academic, 2010.
Anonymous. "New Literature." *The Biblical World* 31.6 (1908) 478–80.
———. "New Literature." *The Biblical World* 33.5 (1909) 356–60.
———. "Work and Workers." *The Biblical World* 25.5 (1905) 393.
Arthurs, Jeffrey D. *Preaching with Variety: How to Re-Create the Dynamics of Biblical Genre*. Grand Rapids: Kregel, 2007.
Augustine. *On Christian Doctrine*. Translated by J. F. Shaw. London: Aeterna, 2014.
Black, David Alan. "Exegesis for the Text-Driven Sermon." In *Text-Driven Preaching: God's Word at the Heart of Every Sermon*, 135–62. Nashville: B&H Academic, 2010.
Blackwood, Andrew Watterson. *Biographical Preaching for Today: The Pulpit Use of Bible Cases*. Nashville: Abingdon, 1954.
———. *Expository Preaching for Today: Case Studies of Bible Passages*. Nashville: Abingdon, 1953.
Block, Daniel I. "Preaching Old Testament Law to New Testament Christians." *Southeastern Theological Review* 3.2 (2012) 195–221.
———. "'That They May All Fear Me': Interpreting and Preaching Hebrew Wisdom." *Journal for Baptist Theology & Ministry* 13.2 (2016) 68–79.
Brown, John. *Puritan Preaching in England: A Study of Past and Present*. New York: Charles Scribner's Sons, 1900.
Calkins, Harold L. *Master Preachers: Their Study and Devotional Habits*. Washington, DC: Review and Herald, 1960.
Carlile, John C. *Alexander Maclaren, D.D.: The Man and His Message*. New York: Funk and Wagnalls, 1902.
Chapell, Bryan. *Christ-Centered Preaching: Redeeming the Expository Sermon*. 2nd ed. Grand Rapids: Baker Academic, 2005.
Chisholm, Jr., Robert B. "Interpreting the Psalms." In *Interpreting the Psalms for Teaching and Preaching*, edited by Herbert W. Bateman, IV and D. Brent Sandy, 16–29. St. Louis: Chalice, 2010.
Choules, John Overton. *The Cruise of the Steam Yacht North Star: A Narrative of the Excursion of Mr. Vanderbilt's Party*. Bedford, MA: Applewood Books, 1854.
Currier, Albert H. *Nine Great Preachers*. Boston: Pilgrim, 1912.

Bibliography

Dargan, Edwin Charles. *A History of Preaching: From the Close of the Reformation Period to the End of the Nineteenth Century, 1572–1900.* Vol. 2. 2 vols. New York: A. C. Armstrong, 1905.

Doriani, Daniel M. *Getting the Message: A Plan for Interpreting and Applying the Bible.* Phillipsburg, NJ: P&R, 1996.

Faunce, W.H.P. "Expository Preaching. III." *The Biblical World* 12.5 (1898) 320–326.

Fee, Gordon D., and Douglas Stuart. *How to Read the Bible for All Its Worth: A Guide to Understanding the Bible.* 2nd ed. Grand Rapids: Zondervan, 1993.

Frame, John M. *The Doctrine of the Christian Life.* A Theology of Lordship. Phillipsburg, NJ: P&R, 2008.

Goldsworthy, Graeme. *Preaching the Whole Bible as Christian Scripture: The Application of Biblical Theology to Expository Preaching.* Grand Rapids: Eerdmans, 2000.

Hamer, F. E. "Dr. Alexander McLaren and Union Chapel, Manchester: The Church, Its Pastor and Its People." *British Monthly* (1900) 31–36.

Hopkins, Mark. "The Down-Grade Controversy." *Christian History* 10.29 (1991). https://christianhistoryinstitute.org/magazine/article/down-grade-controversy/.

Hughes, Graham W. "Union Chapel, Manchester." *Baptist Quarterly* 13.2 (Apr. 1949) 92–93.

Kaiser Jr., Walter C. *Preaching and Teaching from the Old Testament: A Guide for the Church.* Grand Rapids: Baker Academic, 2003.

———. *Toward an Exegetical Theology: Biblical Exegesis for Preaching and Teaching.* Grand Rapids: Baker Academic, 1981.

Köstenberger, Andreas J., and Richard Duane Patterson. *Invitation to Biblical Interpretation: Exploring the Hermeneutical Triad of History, Literature, and Theology.* Grand Rapids: Kregel, 2011.

Kuruvilla, Abraham. *Privilege the Text!: A Theological Hermeneutic for Preaching.* Chicago: Moody, 2013.

Larsen, David L. *The Company of Preachers: A History of Biblical Preaching from the Old Testament to the Modern Era.* Vol. 2. Grand Rapids: Kregel, 1998.

Little, Fergus G. "Historical Registers of Scottish Baptists." *Baptist Quarterly* 24.5 (1972) 229–32.

Long, Thomas G. *Preaching and the Literary Forms of the Bible.* Philadelphia: Fortress, 1989.

Maclaren, Alexander. *After the Resurrection.* New York: Funk & Wagnalls, n.d.

———. *The Best of Alexander MacLaren.* Edited by Gaius Glenn Atkins. London: Hodder and Stoughton, 1950.

———. *The Book of Psalms I—XXXVIII.* Edited by W. Robertson Nicoll. 3rd ed. Vol. 1. 3 vols. The Expositor's Bible. New York: A. C. Armstrong and Son, 1896.

———. *The Book of Psalms XC—CL.* Edited by W. Robertson Nicoll. Vol. 3. 3 vols. The Expositor's Bible. New York: A. C. Armstrong and Son, 1894.

———. *The Book of Psalms XXXIX—LXXXIX.* Edited by W. Robertson Nicoll. Vol. 2. 3 vols. The Expositor's Bible. New York: A. C. Armstrong and Son, 1893.

———. *Christ in the Heart.* New York: Funk & Wagnalls, 1902.

———. *The Conquering Christ and Other Sermons.* London: Sampson Low, Marston & Company, 1891.

———. "Counsels for the Study and the Life." *Review and Expositor* 22.2 (1925) 161–78.

———. *Deuteronomy, Joshua, Judges, Ruth, and First Book of Samuel.* Expositions of Holy Scripture. Grand Rapids: Baker, 1974.

———. *Ephesians*. Expositions of Holy Scripture. Grand Rapids: Baker, 1974.
———. *Epistles to Colossians and Philemon*. The Expositor's Bible. London: Hodder and Stoughton, 1898.
———. *Esther, Job, Proverbs and Ecclesiastes*. Expositions of Holy Scripture. Grand Rapids: Baker, 1974.
———. *Exodus, Leviticus and Numbers*. Expositions of Holy Scripture. Grand Rapids: Baker, 1974.
———. *Expositions of Holy Scripture*. 17 vols. Grand Rapids: Baker, 1974.
———. *Ezekiel, Daniel, and the Minor Prophets*. Expositions of Holy Scripture. Grand Rapids: Baker, 1974.
———. *Genesis*. Expositions of Holy Scripture. Grand Rapids: Baker, 1974.
———. "The Gospel for the Day." In *Baptist Union Papers: 1870–879*, 1–29. London: Yates & Alexander, 1875.
———. "The Inaugural Address." In *Autumnal Session of the Baptist Union*. London: E. Marlborough & Co., 1875.
———. *Isaiah and Jeremiah: Isaiah Chaps. XLIX to End, Jeremiah*. Expositions of Holy Scripture. Grand Rapids: Baker, 1974.
———. *Isaiah: Chaps. I to XLVIII*. Expositions of Holy Scripture. Grand Rapids: Baker, 1974.
———. *Last Sheaves*. New York: Funk & Wagnalls, n.d.
———. *Leaves from the Tree of Life*. New York: Funk & Wagnalls, n.d.
———. *The Life of David as Reflected in the Psalms*. Edinburgh: Macniven & Wallace, 1880.
———. "An Old Preacher on Preaching." In *Report of the Joint Assembly of the Baptist and Congregational Unions, April 23 and 25, 1901: With Illustrative Notes*. 19–40. London: Baptist Tract and Book Society, 1901.
———. *Psalms I to XLIX*. Expositions of Holy Scripture. Grand Rapids: Baker, 1974.
———. *Psalms LI to CXLV*. Expositions of Holy Scripture. Grand Rapids: Baker, 1974.
———. *A Rosary of Christian Graces*. London: Horace Marshall & Son, 1899.
———. *Second Kings from Chapter VIII, and Chronicles, Ezra, and Nehemiah*. Expositions of Holy Scripture. Grand Rapids: Baker, 1974.
———. *Second Samuel and the Books of Kings to Second Kings VII*. Expositions of Holy Scripture. Grand Rapids: Baker, 1974.
———. *The Secret of Power*. New York: Funk & Wagnalls, 1905.
———. *Sermons Preached in Manchester: First Series*. New York: Funk & Wagnalls, 1902.
———. *Sermons Preached in Manchester: Second Series*. New York: Funk & Wagnalls, 1902.
———. *Sermons Preached in Manchester: Third Series*. New York: Funk & Wagnalls, 1902.
———. *The Unchanging Christ*. New York: Funk & Wagnalls, n.d.
———. *Victory in Failure*. Edited by William J. Petersen. New Canaan, CT: Keats, 1980.
———. *The Wearied Christ*. New York: Funk & Wagnalls, n.d.
———. *Week-Day Evening Addresses*. New York: Funk & Wagnalls, 1905.
Majors, James Edgar. "The Foundation for Text-Accurate Applications in Text-Driven Sermons: Systematic Integration of Exposition and Application." D.Min. diss, Southwestern Baptist Theological Seminary, 2014.
Mathewson, Steven D. *The Art of Preaching Old Testament Narrative*. Grand Rapids: Baker Academic, 2002.

Bibliography

McLaren, E. T. *Dr. McLaren of Manchester: A Sketch.* London: Hodder and Stoughton, 1911.

Meyer, F. B. "Alexander Maclaren: An Appreciation." In *Similes and Figures from Alexander Maclaren*, edited by Francis E. Clark, 9–16. New York: Fleming H. Revell, 1910.

Mills, Michael. "Great Preachers and Their Preaching: Alexander Maclaren" *Preaching Source*, 2024. https://equipthecalled.com/ps-article/great-preachers-and-their-preaching-alexander-maclaren/.

Moseley, Allan. *From the Study to the Pulpit: An 8-Step Method for Preaching and Teaching the Old Testament.* Bellingham, WA: Lexham, 2017.

Moyer, Elgin. *Who Was Who in Church History.* Chicago: Moody, 1962.

Nicoll, W. Robertson. *Princes of the Church.* London: Hodder and Stoughton Limited, 1921.

Nogalski, James D. "Recurring Themes in the Book of the Twelve: Creating Points of Contact for a Theological Reading." *Interpretation* 61.2 (2007) 125–36.

Old, Hughes Oliphant. *The Reading and Preaching of Scripture in the Worship of the Christian Church: The Modern Age.* Vol. 6. 7 vols. Grand Rapids: Eerdmans, 2007.

Osborne, Grant R. *The Hermeneutical Spiral: A Comprehensive Introduction to Biblical Interpretation.* Downers Grove, IL: InterVarsity, 2006.

Pace, R. Scott. "Alexander Maclaren: The Art of Hermeneutics for the Practice of Homiletics." In *A Legacy of Preaching: Enlightenment to the Present Day*, edited by Benjamin K. Forrest, et al., 2:70–87. Grand Rapids: Zondervan, 2018.

Patrick, Johnstone G. "A Prince of Preachers: A Jubilee Tribute to Dr. Alexander Maclaren." *Life of Faith*, Feb. 7, 1976.

Pattison, T. Harwood. *The History of Christian Preaching.* Philadelphia: American Baptist Publication Society, 1903.

Pitts, John. "Alexander Maclaren: Monarch of the Pulpit." *Christianity Today* 8.18 (1964) 7–9.

Ralston, Timothy J. "Preaching the Psalms: Sermonic Forms." In *Interpreting the Psalms for Teaching and Preaching*, edited by Herbert W. Bateman, IV and D. Brent Sandy, 30–44. St. Louis: Chalice, 2010.

Robinson, Haddon. "The Heresy of Application." *Christianity Today*, 1997. https://www.christianitytoday.com/pastors/1997/fall/7l4o2o.html.

Sandy, D. Brent, and Tiberius Rata. "Approaching the Psalms." In *Interpreting the Psalms for Teaching and Preaching*, edited by Herbert W. Bateman, IV and D. Brent Sandy, 2–15. St. Louis: Chalice, 2010.

Sellers, Ian. "Other Times, Other Ministries: John Fawcett and Alexander McLaren." *Baptist Quarterly* 32.4 (Oct. 1987) 181–99.

Smith, Steven W. *Recapturing the Voice of God: Shaping Sermons like Scripture.* Nashville: B&H Academic, 2015.

Stewart, James Stuart. "Dr. Alexander Maclaren: The Prince of Biblical Expositors." *Review and Expositor* 8.1 (1911) 32–50.

Stott, John R.W. *Between Two Worlds: The Art of Preaching in the Twentieth Century.* Grand Rapids: Eerdmans, 1982.

Taylor, John Phelps. "The Psalms, v 1: Psalms 1–38." *Andover Review* 19.112 (1893) 496–97.

Vines, Jerry, and Jim Shaddix. *Power in the Pulpit: How to Prepare and Deliver Expository Sermons.* Chicago: Moody, 1999.

Bibliography

Walker, C. Kyle. *Let the Text Talk: Preaching That Treats the Text on Its Own Terms*. Fort Worth: Seminary Hill Press, 2018.

Webber, F. R. *A History of Preaching in Britain and America: Including the Biographies of Many Princes of the Pulpit and the Men Who Influenced Them*. Milwaukee: Northwestern, 1952.

Wiersbe, Warren W. *50 People Every Christian Should Know: Learning from Spiritual Giants of the Faith*. Grand Rapids: Baker Books, 2009.

———. *Walking with the Giants: A Minister's Guide to Good Reading and Great Preaching*. Grand Rapids: Baker, 1976.

Wilkinson, William Cleaver. *Modern Masters of Pulpit Discourse*. New York: Funk & Wagnalls, 1905.

Williamson, David. *The Life of Alexander Maclaren: Preacher and Expositor*. London: James Clarke and Co, 1930.

Wimberly, C. F. *Modern Apostles of Faith*. Nashville: Cokesbury, 1930.

www.ingramcontent.com/pod-product-compliance
Lightning Source LLC
Chambersburg PA
CBHW051108160426
43193CB00010B/1365